Living Inspirit

The Quiet Light Revolution

When you follow the path of meditation and
healing, you create a life worth living.

JENNIFER KITE

BALBOA.
PRESS

A DIVISION OF HAY HOUSE

Balboa Press books may be ordered through booksellers or by contacting:

Balboa Press
A Division of Hay House
1663 Liberty Drive
Bloomington, IN 47403
www.balboapress.com.au
1 (877) 407-4847

Print information available on the last page.

ISBN: 978-1-5043-1687-3 (sc)
ISBN: 978-1-5043-1688-0 (e)

Balboa Press rev. date: 07/17/2019

Contents

Foreword vii
Introduction ix

Part 1: Calling All Light Workers

1. Our Garden of Eden..1
2. The Journey of Life...6
3. The Journey Within...11
4. The Circle of Life 16
5. The Karmic Construct: Bursting the Karma Bubble 24
6. Eliminating Fear...32

Part 2: Finding Your Lost Self

7. The Journey to Love 41
8. The Way in Is Well Lit...49
9. Enlisting Help from Our Spirit Guides 54
10. Light Will Protect..70
11. The Healing Path, Through Meditation.........................76
12. Using Light and Love to Heal...................................91
13. The Chakra System 95
14. Embracing the Child...109
15. Spiritual Housework: Helping Ourselves and Mother Earth........124
16. Fertile Ground 129

Part 3: Light Working!

17. Choosing Goodness...139
18. Growing Your Soul Self..144
19. Joy and Happiness...157
20. Living Inspirit...161

Foreword

A Book of Energy, Healing and Light

I was fortunate to meet Jenny several years ago, when I popped into her practice on the South Coast of New South Wales. Having had my interest piqued, and following many lengthy discussions about the work that Jenny was doing, I chose to explore it further. After the passing of my mum a few years prior, a few sessions with Jenny assisted me in dealing with the many deep feelings which had arisen as a result of this event. I was also fortunate to be offered the opportunity of attending several classes presented by Jenny, encompassing the various aspects of her work, making me very inspired to practice what I had learnt. In so doing, I found great consolation and assistance in dealing with the everyday travails with which many of us may be confronted. In my case in particular, the practice of guided meditations was invaluable in assisting me in my recovery from aggressive chemotherapy and the passing of my husband. Implementing the various strategies learnt has assisted in my living a more reflective and fulfilling life. *Living InSpirit* is an engaging read, which contains explanations, inspirational examples, and practical ideas to encourage engagement and thoughtful reflection, offering the potential for significantly enhancing the lives of those who read this inspirational book. I highly recommend this easily read and understood book to those who are aspiring to make their everyday lives flow more freely and easily.

Lesley Maxwell
MEd, DipTeach

Introduction

I am here to help. I wish to share what I know to be true. Many souls inhabiting the earth at this time are here under a veil and are living lives of confusion and fear. I believe that knowledge takes the place of fear. Knowledge and understanding give hope. The purpose of this book is to bring forth a clear understanding of the circumstances that shape your world and to offer guidance and instructions to facilitate your journey. I hope my words will uplift your soul and open your mind to new understandings and new concepts. I believe the spiritual path is the only way forward and that this path will open your heart towards absolute love of self and love for others. *Living Inspirit* can be your own inspiration for positive change.

The journey home is our primary goal. The day we took our first breath signalled the beginning of yet another life experience which would ultimately bring us back to ourselves and to the Creator. All of us involved in the writing of this book have lived lives on earth and breathed the air that you now breathe. We have participated in all aspects of living, and we have experienced the horrors and the joys that life on earth has to offer. It is because of this real connection to this dense field of learning that we know we can offer you understanding and hope. The journey home to the source of our souls—must be the primary goal for all of us.

I have been working under the loving guidance of my spirit guides for many years. I have become a conscious channel for spiritual teachings, and I offer words of advice and encouragement to my many clients.

Through my belief in myself and my faith in the Divine Creator, I have persisted even when at times I found life extremely difficult. I have been dedicated to learning, and my thirst for knowledge has brought me to this place today.

The extraordinary connection to my spirit guide and higher self has enabled me to work through my personal lessons of spiritual growth. Over time I have healed many aspects of my life and learned to love and acknowledge my divinity on every level of my existence. I have become fully self-aware and understand my deepest needs and my life purpose. I am so grateful for the commitment and courage I receive from my higher self in the pursuit of truth. My commitment and dedication to healing and the path of light are an inspiration from this divine being. My words are from the heart and are channelled from my higher self.

I am a wife, mother, sister, daughter, and friend. I am also a spiritual counsellor, healer, and teacher. I have come to accept the good and the bad in my life as gifts with which to grow and learn. My life has been clearly defined by my relationships and roles, and I have also come to accept that, within the structure of love and family, my true purpose here on earth is one of teacher and healer. The challenges we all face in life have not missed me, but I have learned to love my life and my soul journey here on earth at this time.

I have tried to bring compassion and understanding into every relationship I have been part of and every role I have embraced. I have guided and supported my loved ones on their journeys as well as offered support and guidance to people within my circle of influence. As many women do, I have focused much of my time and energy over the years on raising my children and supporting my husband and family in any way I could. There came a time, however, that in order to do this effectively I had to accept, love, and nurture myself as well.

So herein lies the purpose of this book. I offer you the opportunity to align with your spiritual essence and make your life a joy. By bringing light into every aspect of your life, you will have a more purposeful and satisfying journey this time around.

A very long time ago, I was sitting in quiet meditation one day, struggling to find my purpose in life. I was asking the universe possibly the most-asked question on the planet: What is my true purpose? What am I doing here? I stopped struggling for a moment, and in the silence I heard the words "unconditional love of self." These softly spoken words resonated with me, and I realised that I needed to learn how to do this. I shrugged my shoulders and thought about the meaning of these words for a time; then I went about my day. I did not understand the profound nature of this message until many years later.

I began my personal journey of introspection at a very early age. By nature I was curious and observant. I questioned my reality, and I questioned the world I lived in. I noticed what went on around me. Interestingly, one of my favourite books as a child was a large hardcover publication, full of facts, called *Tell Me Why*. This was my personal mantra and defined my years at school. I questioned my teachers and my parents. When their answers did not satisfy my quest for truth, I turned my attention to self-education, and books became my teachers.

Sitting in front of my bookshelf, I would decide what to read or reread. Keeping my bookshelf tidy and ordered was one of my daily joys. My books of choice were adventure stories and make-believe, but I always enjoyed books about my world or those that answered my questions about life.

I was the second-born daughter in a family of four girls. My parents are nonpracticing Catholics, and it was inevitable that the four of us went to a catholic girls' school. It was here that we received our first spiritual lessons. A broad education was also a critical issue, particularly for our father. My sisters and I spent twelve years at this school, and the education I received there contributed immensely to the person I am today.

Underlying most of our classes was the religious influence of the Catholic Church. Every subject area was directly or indirectly influenced by the rules and teachings of the Vatican. The discipline at school was quite harsh and the expectations towards behaviour and academic achievement very high. I was at school during the 1960s and 70s, and from my recent observations as a primary schoolteacher, I have noted that times have changed in many ways—for the better.

Although not the *best years* of my life, I now see these years at school as a gift. At times I found the system of education stifling, dogmatic, or unjust—and on occasion completely illogical. My questioning of the rules, inconsistencies, and religious doctrine got me into lots of trouble over the years. The nuns at our school were very freewheeling with feather dusters and wooden rulers. However, my having a natural sense of humour and wonderful friends helped lessen the negative impact of everyday issues at school.

One day when I was in my first year of high school, I took a very controversial newspaper clipping into my religion class. The article was only small; I had found it the day before while glancing through the Sunday papers. The article talked about the possibility that Jesus and Mary Magdalene had been married. Researchers had come upon some quite convincing information and released this news to the press. Now, in retrospect, I realise that it would have been during the time the Nag Hammadi texts and Gnostic Gospels were being researched and publicly aired.

Bringing that newspaper clipping into my class was a very big mistake. My teacher came at me with a ruler, in a fit of anger and hysteria. She hit me at the back of my head and tore the article out of my hand. I know I didn't go to class that day with the intention of upsetting her; I took in the article as a point of interest that might lead to discussion.

I was twelve years old and had already begun opening my world up to an infinite number of truths and possibilities.

During my years at school, there were some truly wonderful souls who would stand before us in class and demonstrate the beauty of faith, grace, and love. Teachers such as these inspired me towards an undying faith in the Creator and all things spiritual. These wonderful women were rare within this system, but I thank them for their dedication and love of teaching.

My search for the meaning of life was well under way by the time I left school and began my study at teacher's college. My learning was also inspired by my travels; I spent my early twenties visiting many obscure and fascinating overseas destinations. I backpacked overland from Singapore through Thailand, Nepal, India, Pakistan, Afghanistan, Iran, Turkey, and on to Greece and Europe. I travelled with a friend and met an incredible range of interesting, intrepid travellers. I visited countries that are now off limits to the average tourist. I look back at my travels and realise that I was guided to many ancient cities and towns for a reason. I also see now how protected I was by my spirit guide, even though I was not aware of his presence at the time.

Many years later I was reading a book on meditation. The author spoke in depth of spirit guides and how they are dedicated to us and our journeys here on earth. To read that we each have a spirit guide who is dedicated to our well-being was very overwhelming but also exciting. The thought of this took me back to my early years in kindergarten, where we were taught about angels, guardian angels. I decided it was time to meet my guide, and through the process of meditation I did. This process allowed me to build an energetic bridge of communication with my own spirit guide. I persisted over a brief period of time, and after many attempts at trying to relax and not think but just breathe, it finally happened one day, with surprising ease.

In my meditative state, my guide, Christopher, presented himself, smiling at me from under a tree in a magnificent garden. I was overwhelmed with emotions, and I found it difficult to believe this being of light was dedicated to me and my personal journey. My feelings of unworthiness were very close to the surface at that time of my life. My spiritual journey of self-knowledge and love had only just begun. Ever since that first meeting, Christopher has helped me to learn and study about life and spirituality at the pace that has been perfect for me.

Through his guidance I have broadened my perspective by reading books on metaphysics and spirituality. I have read about alternative world histories as well as accepted ones. I have read about reincarnation, meditation, and learning to love. I have read about ancient civilisations and ancient religions. I have read about angels, and I have read about ghosts. I have read the stories of inspiring men and women who have walked this earth. I have read and researched the extra-terrestrial (ET) phenomenon as well as the worst of human behaviour displayed by individuals and nations.

My intention was always to know the truth. My study will continue as long as I exist here on earth. Knowledge is liberating and empowering. It is essential to know what kind of world we live in so that we can live our lives well. Thus I educated myself; with the help of Christopher and with his further guidance, I turned my search inwards through the practice of meditation.

This journey within has been my biggest source of learning and knowledge. It has raised my awareness so that I can see the bigger picture, see where I fit into the canvas. With introspection, I have learned who I am and why I am here. I have connected to my higher self and now know my true purpose. I discovered on this journey of self-awareness that the world we live in is created in every moment of every day by our thoughts, words, and actions. Thus, to live a purposeful and joyful life, I must take absolute responsibility for it on all levels.

This was a difficult reality to accept and understand, because it has always been easier to blame others for our personal heartaches and misfortunes. It is a lot easier to hand that responsibility over to a parent, sibling, or authority figure. For me to realise that I was at the steering wheel, driving the car, was quite challenging—and yet at the same time encouraging. Blame became futile; forgiveness took its place.

I had to forgive myself as well as others.

Through my spiritual connection I have travelled the road of personal healing and empowerment. I have come to understand the importance of self-knowledge as well as self-love. I have personally experienced how this energy connects us to the Divine Source of love and brings this wonderful sustaining energy into our lives—forever.

I believe that I am here to help teach people how to love and accept themselves and, within this energy, to love and accept others. I believe that by bringing people back to their Divine Source I will help them understand the power of love. They will recognise that through personal healing they can access this love, to bring fulfilment and purpose to life.

Unconditional love and acceptance of ourselves and all people is paramount to our journeys. Our spirit guides and higher selves are committed to inspiring us and guiding us towards this ultimate goal. Self-love becomes the vehicle for our journey home to the Creator.

As we align with the power of our higher selves, we will also align with humility, compassion, and loving acceptance of others. It becomes essential, therefore, that those of us who choose to step onto this path of light do so with the highest intentions for the evolution of humanity and Mother Earth.

It takes an enormous amount of courage, conviction, and commitment to leave our divine home and live a life here on earth. Our roles are clearly defined in this physical dimension, and the sooner we know our true purpose, the sooner we can take over the steering wheel of our life and live it to the fullest. Through lifetime after lifetime we move closer to a required goal of spiritual mastery. With this growth and learning, we then move closer to the divine source of all life.

The magnificence of the gesture by each individual soul to live out a life here on earth is matched by the magnificence of our higher selves. We are held in very high esteem by the spiritual beings who support each of our incarnations. We are honoured and applauded because of our courage and dedication to the journey and to the evolution of humanity. This is why we have such trusted and supportive guidance on the other side. We do not have to do any of this alone.

Beyond the veil, in the next dimension, stand our spirit guides. These loving souls know us better than we could ever possibly know ourselves. They were with us at the time we planned our lives, and they remain conscious of our sacred contracts and plans when we do not. Getting to know our spirit guides and accessing their wisdom and grace is the most profound way we can move forward on our paths and fulfil our spiritual destinies.

This book will allow you to open the door to the ultimate you. You will come to understand the need to identify your authentic self. Once identified, you can grow to a place of unconditional acceptance and love of self.

We were all born perfect! We came to this earth in perfect time, in perfect order. We exist in the divine order of things, and to reconnect to this perfection, it is necessary to learn about our journeys and the reasons we are here.

This book is about self-empowerment, self-awareness, and self-love. To know ourselves is to love ourselves. To understand is to accept. With this deep understanding and clarity, it is possible to accept and love our lives. The spiritual self exists within each of us. This spiritual self is the courageous soul that embarked on this journey many, many lifetimes ago. When we get in touch with our spirits, it is possible to reclaim the courage, hope and trust we were born with.

Let us step forward and allow our spiritual selves to take charge of our lives again. This is the self-empowerment I speak of. It's the self-awareness, understanding, and love that comes with the journey of life.

My purpose as a spiritual teacher and healer is to guide individuals along a path of self-discovery, where they learn to love their authentic selves and gain access to their spirit guides and higher selves.

Many years ago I enrolled in a series of lessons which opened me up to the true nature of the universe and my connection to the Divine Creator. This course was based on parapsychology and metaphysics. It challenged all my traditional beliefs and forced me to account for my life, thereby bringing my ego-self into line with my divine energy. With this information and my connection to the source of all knowledge through my higher self, I decided to share what I know to be true.

I have personally walked this path of healing, and I bring these words to you from my higher self, John, in conjunction with the wisdom and teaching of my spiritual guides. I see myself as a conduit of loving teachings and wisdom, all of which are on offer to those who are open and receptive to spiritual growth. My intention is to help my earthly companions find the love and joy that they deserve and that is available to all.

My life has been blessed in many ways. My husband and I married in 1981and have raised four remarkable, healthy children. Our loving family is at the centre of our world! Being born in Sydney in the 1950s and spending most weekends on Bondi Beach, I know how blessed I have been. During my lifetime I have endeavoured to bring myself to a place of gratitude, peace, and harmony. It has not always been easy, but my faith in the divine plan has kept me going.

I remember back to when I was eight years old. I felt sad and unhappy, which was incongruent with the life I was living. My sisters and I were being raised in an affluent home. Dad was a businessman and our mother was a stay-at-home mum. We enjoyed holidays in the snow and at the beach. Our birthdays were always fun, and Christmas was an exciting time for all. However, within this seemingly perfect world, I felt something was missing. I often prayed to Jesus to take me "home." Deep inside I ached for the unconditional love I remembered, a love so grand and expansive! I missed it terribly. At the time I did not understand what made me so unhappy. Now, with the passage of time and with the opportunity for spiritual learning, I have identified and rediscovered the love I craved.

It was during these years that I first began to read. I read anything I could get my hands on. Firstly, books took me into worlds of fantasy, adventure, and suspense. Secondly, apart from school, they were the source of my education. Books allowed me to escape my unhappiness and my feelings of wretchedness and at the same time answered many of my questions about life.

I became responsible for my own happiness for the first time in my life. My interest in books led me to view the world from many different perspectives and ultimately to question the reality of my life and the reality of the lives of those around me.

Now, after many years of personal healing, study, and spiritual growth, I have moved into the space that resonates truth and love. In this personal space, I first contacted my higher self, John. Through my alignment with Christopher, John came to me in meditation; he has been guiding and teaching me ever since. Even this experience was difficult for me to believe at times, as I was challenged by my own lower self and by the doubts of others.

I owe everything to my higher self-connection. It is through this connection to the highest vibration of me that I have gained deep clarity and purpose. It is through this connection that I found the courage and the determination to bring this book to fruition. I trust that whoever reads this book is in the right place at the right time and, in their own way, will benefit humanity because they exist.

I dedicate this book, in chronological order, to my parents, my sisters, my husband, and my children. I thank the Divine Creator for this opportunity to live a life of purpose and passion. I pray that, through my work, John's wisdom and loving healing energy will once again flow through the hearts of many.

This book is a collection of thoughts, ideas, and personal experiences that will help raise your awareness of how the path to spirituality can be simple, easily attained, and yet profoundly life-changing.

I wish to acknowledge and thank my family, friends, and teachers. Each one of you is a gift from God. I am forever grateful and honoured to share this journey with you all.

I also wish to acknowledge the courageous souls who come into my healing practice because someone said to each of them, "You need to see Jenny." Some new clients step in nervous and unsure, but the common thread among these souls is that they truly want to become better people. They want healing, hope, and purpose. Sometimes they just need to be heard, and when they become aligned with their spirit guides, they have loving shoulders to lean on and open hearts to trust forever.

In my healing practice I engage with the higher-self realm and the spirit guides, to clear and balance the energy of each client in order to open the pathway to spirit. I wish to thank my clients for the love and respect they show me as well as the lessons offered to me from them and their higher selves.

I will always be a student of the light and will share what I know and learn on this journey with others.

As a spiritual counsellor, I have had the opportunity to teach others and guide them forward. My knowledge has been gleaned from other teachers, my metaphysical studies, my healing practice, and through my personal meditation process.

If this book has fallen into your hands, by whatever means, I have already assumed you are looking to improve your personal circumstances through a connection to spirit and self-love.

Prior knowledge of the spiritual realm and meditation is not necessary, but there are a few things I would like to clarify and explain before we go any further. The following concepts will all be explained more fully throughout the book, but for now, here is a small window into our world.

However you view and understand God to be, feel free to apply your title. My understanding is that we carry the light of creation within every cell of our bodies, and this light is the life force of our creator. It is both male and female in origin. My understanding is that life on earth is lovingly supported by a benevolent energy that is home to our souls. I have referred to God as the Divine Creator, the Goddess, the Universe, and All that Is. It is important that you accept that there is a force bigger than ourselves and that this force is all-loving.

In addition to this, you need to be open to the concepts of spirit and the multidimensional planes of existence.

The concept of reincarnation will help you to adjust your thinking about the journey of your soul and life beyond the physical plane. Reincarnation means that your soul will come into different bodies, both male and female, at various times, for different life experiences and lessons. In this way, with life after life, the soul will grow in love, awareness, knowledge, and light, until it reaches the state of perfection that allows it to return home to the Divine Creator, and the cycle of reincarnation ceases.

The higher self is the aspect of our soul that stays connected to the Creator while we reincarnate on earth. It is pure love and is the highest vibration that our earthly bodies can be aligned with while living out our lives. While we are on earth, the connection to the higher self can only be made through the pathway of personal healing, love, and light.

Spirit guides are our nonphysical earthly companions. Each of us has the blessing of a spirit guide who has agreed to journey to earth with us and guide us through our current incarnations. Spirit guides know our soul contracts and life plans. They also filter the energy of our higher selves through the vibration of love and light.

When a person dies, he or she is lovingly guided back to the heavenly home with the assistance of the spirit guide and the angelic realm. If this system goes down, a soul may miss its opportunity to cross over to the higher planes of existence. It then becomes stuck in the physical realm, becoming lost. Lost souls stay earthbound through the energy matrix of the living, and they attach themselves to familiar surroundings and people. When this happens, the soul cannot move on and reincarnate again, so its spiritual journey becomes blocked.

The *chakra system* is the term used for the energy centres within the physical body that keep the life force flowing and vital. The term *chakra* is a Sanskrit word that is now widely used to describe these vital energy centres. The soul enters the embryonic state of the person and aligns within the chakra system, anchoring the soul self within the physical body. The chakra system supports all life from this point on. This energy system becomes the gateway to physical, emotional, and spiritual healing. This then aligns with the pathway to love and light.

For over twelve years I have been teaching meditation classes and spiritual development. I have been fortunate to witness the personal and spiritual growth in many, many people. I have seen first-hand healing in relationships and improvement in health. As members of my classes embraced meditation practice, the world they lived in changed in all manner of ways. Almost every class member faced challenges; this is because change is a challenge in itself.

Over time and with a commitment to love and light, progress was made. Each class was unique and extraordinarily special. I have met some remarkable people on my journey and am grateful to all of them for what they brought to the group and shared. The outcomes for each individual depended on their input, and in most cases enormous progress was made because of their courage, positive attitudes, and demonstration of faith!

I pray that this book reaches many intrepid souls who wish to make changes in their lives. Within this book lie the blueprint and roadmap for such change.

Part 1

Calling All Light Workers

1

Never doubt that a small group of committed citizens can change the world; indeed, it's the only thing that ever has.

MARGARET MEAD
(1901–1978, AMERICAN CULTURAL ANTHROPOLOGIST, AUTHOR, AND SPEAKER)

Our Garden of Eden

Traditionally, the Garden of Eden engenders images of a magical, mystical, and promising land. Ancient stories have told us, however, that it is also a place of deception, sadness, scarcity, and struggle.

Our world exists in a dimension and space that separate us from the spiritual world. This veil of separation is thin, and as we move into the future, other dimensions within our planetary system are becoming more accessible. The entire vibration of Planet Earth is in the process of changing and shifting. As the changes occur and the vibration of Planet Earth moves higher, the veil will become finer.

A planetary *ascension* is being heralded at this time in our evolution. This is significant, because it denotes a new time for humanity and advancement on a spiritual and energetic level. The ascension of our planetary home means that the vibration of earth is increasing. However, this advancement can only be manifested through the energy of love, nurture, and sustenance for Mother Earth and her inhabitants.

Earth is our Garden of Eden, where souls come to grow. Due to circumstances and life choices, souls sometimes live in undernourished soil, with no light or hope, so these souls simply manage to survive for a time. Other souls find themselves planted in sunny, open fields of light, warmth, and fertile soil. Under these circumstances, souls can blossom and grow.

The range of life experiences in our Garden of Eden moves from lack to abundance, from sadness to joy, and from grief to hope. Much of what we struggle for is personal power and the right to simply exist. From the moment we arrive, we are helpless infants, totally dependent upon our parents and family for physical nurturing and survival. The quality of life and the endurance of the soul are reflective of these early childhood years.

Our real and authentic power, however, lies within our spiritual energy and our connection to our soul selves. If we have struggled for light, nourishment, and survival, our souls exist within a state of self-imposed powerlessness, based on what we believe and expect about ourselves.

The Garden of Eden we live in has become a contrasting landscape, a place of duality. There exist the muddy compost heaps of life's rotting castoffs as well as the magnificent, tall, and generous trees of ancient and lush forests that provide shelter and security. Wherever we choose to take root in this garden will affect the outcome of our personal growth and soul journeys. The higher the quality of our soil and conditions, the more likely we are to reach our true potential in this world.

Within our soul energy, our own Garden of Eden exists, and we have the power to live in this energy in whatever way we choose. If our belief systems support our authentic selves, then our lives become wonderful healthy expressions of our souls. However, if we believe that we are unworthy or to blame, then our garden will be an expression of this untruth in an unpleasant reality.

Gardens represent the energy of renewal, death, longevity, survival, resilience, and beauty. As all of us move towards a new global energy, a higher vibration, we must become accountable for our actions of the past, present, and future. As a race of beings, we humans are now seeing who is most resilient, whose life structure supports longevity, and who is accountable for his or her spiritual earthly direction.

Our Creator provided this wonderful, abundant garden for us to grow in. It is desired and hoped that we grow our hearts in unconditional love and acceptance for ourselves and others. We have an unlimited array of resources and get to choose our circumstances. So you'd think the plan would meet with enormous success—yet this world seems to be more difficult to live in than ever before.

As you look around you and see the colour green, know that this colour is a gift from our creator. Green is the colour of our heart centre, and this vibration resonates at the vibration of love energy. Now look around again, and notice the grass that you walk on, the trees that give you shade, the forests, and the leaves. This green is a daily reminder of how much we are loved and supported by our creator. This colour exists within each of us, in our hearts. Again, this is another example of how we are being taken care of, how much we are loved.

Nature exists in its beauty as a reflection of the power, intelligence, and divine design of the Creator. The vibrant green is a reflection of the unconditional love here amongst us. It is a constant reminder that we exist in the divine plan, that we exist in love, whether we are conscious of it or not.

Think now about the power you hold in your hands, including the power to grow this love energy within your heart as well as the power to deny it. Denial of love withers the soul of the individual in the same way that the destruction of our vast natural resources withers the soul of the planet. Growing love within our own hearts creates a ripple effect that spreads to others and to our home, Planet Earth.

Spirituality is simply becoming aware that we are not here alone, we have not been abandoned, and we have not been forgotten. We began our soul journeys on this planet many, many lifetimes ago. Our initial step down was a courageous and hopeful stride.

Many of us have enjoyed lifetimes of pure joy and delight, but to understand the entire soul purpose, it is important to experience life first-hand, so we can develop empathy and compassion towards others as well as loving acceptance of ourselves. These valuable traits will fuel our journeys back to the seat of creation—the seat of absolute and unconditional love.

One's soul can be likened to an enormous ancient tree. It became dislodged from its source eons ago in the form of a seed. Through the perfection of creation and the energy of the universe, it moved away from its source and eventually found a place to grow. The Garden of Eden, the earth school, is that place. To grow back into its original form, it must suffer the ravages of wind and cold as well as the blessings of sunlight and rain.

The elements of nature can at times be difficult to endure, but eventually, the seed grows into a sapling and the sapling into a tree, and with time, the tree grows into a shining example of God at work. It holds within its leaves and branches the life experiences it took to grow and mature. Now the tree can stand as a protective provider of shelter and wisdom, aligned for eternity with creation.

The journey of the soul stands alongside the ancient tree in our Garden of Eden. There is an element of random experiences that shape its growth, but much of what a soul learns is well planned in advance. There are essential life experiences that a soul needs to understand in order to know about the human experience. The more a soul chooses to learn, the more evolved it becomes. Herein lies the wisdom; herein lies the acceptance and love.

Within each and every one of us is a flame of Christ consciousness. This flame is our life force. It cannot be completely distinguished, yet it can be dimmed. As our souls move through the cycle of reincarnation, some lives are lived in more light than others. The planning and choosing are always relevant to the lessons that we need to learn.

Reconnecting to our spiritual energy and soul experience is simply a matter of choice. Once we make the decision to learn more about ourselves, we will feel the energy of support and help around you.

Let's now go within the Garden of Eden, into our own private universe.

There is nothing to fear but fear itself.

FRANKLIN D. ROOSEVELT
(1882–1945, AMERICAN POLITICAL LEADER AND PRESIDENT,)

The Journey of Life

Every person who has existed on this planet is an integral part of the divine plan. Each soul is worthy of love. Each soul is worthy of happiness. The road is marked clearly from the very beginning, and the goal for each soul's incarnation is to experience a life full of joy, success, and purpose. Unfortunately, there are many reasons why this does not happen. The distractions are endless. The nature of the world as we know it drags people away from their true spirits and their potential for happiness and joy.

I was recently walking along the white sands of my favourite beach, which is one of the major blessings of living on the coast! As I looked out over the bay, I noticed the silver light of the early morning sun glistening over the water. It was clear to me that this light was spreading across the bay as the sun rose higher in the morning sky. I was struck by the knowingness that so, too, is the light of the Divine Creator spreading over this planet. There will always be dark pockets where humanity is struggling to exist within the negativity of fear, powerlessness, and ignorance. Yet as I looked out over this pristine bay, I felt good and hopeful about my journey and the evolution of our world.

I use my early morning walks to open up to and communicate with my higher self and guides. The peaceful solitude that the beach provides allows me to access my inner wisdom in a loving and supportive way. I feel that the energy of the beach and ocean helps to create a state of balance and harmony within me that enables a clear transfer of information and learning.

On this particular morning, I raised the subject of fear and negativity. I knew that the words that flowed through me were from my higher self, John. I was told that the true danger to one's spirit does not come from the dark entities that inhabit this planet; the dangers we encounter on this earth spring from internal fear and hatred. The darker side of humanity feeds off this fear and so perpetuates the existence of evil.

When I asked John who his enemies were, he replied, "I do not have enemies, only teachers."

If we are the source of fear, and we attract the negative experiences ourselves, what can we do to protect ourselves and our loved ones?

"Fear is an illusion created by doubt, mistrust, ignorance, negative imaginings, and despairing expectations. The source of these negative emotions and feelings is deep inside us. Underneath jealousy, envy, anger, and contempt lies the root of the problem: self-hatred and loathing. These deep, dark emotions and feelings are projected into the world, creating a reality of fear and negativity. The darker side of our world feeds off this low vibration and causes the situation to grow worse."

The iconic statement, "There is nothing to fear except fear itself" makes perfect sense in the light of this understanding. Fear is created by our thoughts and feelings and becomes intensified and dangerous when projected into the universal consciousness. If like energy attracts like energy, then good, positive thoughts must attract good energy. So, what are we thinking?

"All we are is the result of what we have thought. The mind is everything. What we think we become" (Buddha, sixth to fourth century BCE).

We all exist within a bubble of energy called the *auric field*. Within this energy field exists the duality of dark and light, positive and negative. We as individuals are in control of our lives, and we create our futures according to our thoughts, actions, expectations, and intentions.

It seems obvious to me that we all need to start owning our thoughts, feelings, and emotions. It is time that we understood what it is that we fear and make inroads into dispelling this negative illusion, which is crippling our journey into the light. I know the way forward is through self-love and acceptance. Learning dispels ignorance, and knowledge is the first tool of self-empowerment. Once we learn about ourselves, we can shine a light on what we fear and replace fear with trust. We need to trust the true nature of our own divinity.

Once again my morning walk was proving to be a wonderful learning experience for me. I came to understand that those people who inhabit this world in an extremely dark and violent manner do so because of the volcanoes of self-hatred they hold within their psyches. This energy is then projected into our world through murderous actions, violence against women and children, and religious and political wars. This tide of violence needs to be stopped at the source. Healing the anger, pain, and disempowerment of the disenfranchised will help.

"Holding on to anger is like holding on to a hot coal with the intent of throwing it at someone else; you are the one who gets burned" (Buddha).

When you consciously raise your energy, the light grows within. The way you feel about yourself is immediately reflected within your circle of influence, and then, like the pebble in the stream, these positive feelings move out to affect global consciousness. You can make a positive impact on others in your family and community simply by changing your attitude towards yourself and honouring your path and life.

Whoever we are and whatever we do, we can have a positive impact on the world around us. We are all energetically linked, and what impacts someone on the other side of the world can impact us. As we look around, we witness catastrophes, devastation, grief, sadness, loss, betrayal, deceit, violence, and hatred. On a global scale, we can feel completely disempowered and unable to make a difference. So we ask ourselves, "What can I do?"

There is so much that we can do—this is part of the reason we are here in the first place! By bringing the focus back to self, working with light and love, we can heal and regenerate our own private universe; we can make real and positive changes. This hopeful and positive change on a personal level is where it all begins. By planting seeds of hope, commitment, positive intent, and great expectations, we can fertilise the gardens of our souls and the souls of others.

The power within each of us—the power to make a difference to our own lives and the lives of others—is potent and real. When like-minded souls join with a singular purpose of intent, such as praying for victims of a particular disaster, energetic mountains can be moved.

Our sacred contracts are complex and layered, but our purposes do not require us to be global warriors for peace or environmental saviours. Thanks to the divine universal plan, there are already global warriors, environmental saviours, scientists, healers, humanitarians, and light workers present in our time who are supporting the evolution of our planet. They have chosen their paths, and we must be grateful to them. With our conscious support and gratitude, we can assist them in maintaining their energy and focus.

Those of us living a simpler life can best assist humanity by loving ourselves and our families and by protecting and guiding those closest to us. When we view the disasters on television or are, indeed, involved in one, we can extend a hand of generosity or a heart filled with compassion, and we will make a difference.

Watching commercials for humanitarian causes and feeling useless as I watched the World Trade Centre collapse in 2001 inspired me to gather my resources and meditate my way to a better future. If I could change from within and help others do the same, then maybe, just maybe, we could impact our light and love in positive and profound ways on the world around us.

When we tap into the universal source of light and love, this energy becomes grounded in our hearts and in the planet. As we learn to accept the best that life can offer, we are also assisting the planet to move forward. We can all become vehicles of light and love and circulate this energy around the globe for the good of all. It is important simply to start.

3

Plan for the future, because that is where you
are going to spend the rest of your life.

———

MARK TWAIN
(1835–1910, AMERICAN AUTHOR)

The Journey Within

The journey back to one's authentic self can be a daunting prospect.
The process of moving forward into self-love requires a person to
acknowledge his or her true self in an honest and open way. The
shadow self needs love too. Taking an honest look at past actions,
thoughts, and feelings can create justified anxiety within a person
who understands that we are all ultimately accountable for our words,
actions, and thoughts. Taking ownership and accountability for all
the bad deeds, hateful thoughts, and negative feelings he has had can
cause a person to stop any inward journey of self-discovery.

This is when we need to access the support and love of our spiritual
teachers and guides. We can too easily rationalise negative actions
and keep ourselves locked into a pattern of negative experiences

and despair. The cycle of negativity is self-sustaining, as we slide down the vibrational scale of life. Forgiveness is an energy aligned with unconditional love. If we can summon the energy to forgive ourselves, as well as others, the energy of forgiveness will flow in, fertilising the ground with positive energy that allows for the growth of unconditional love of self.

Our sense of personal value, our self-worth, will determine how much love and goodness we are prepared to accept and enjoy. True courage and faith in the divine plan will help. Many people have journeyed on the path of enlightenment after suffering barbaric times at the hands of others. Victims of crimes have forgiven their tormentors, and political refugees have escaped terrible times and learned to live again. Nelson Mandela was able to forgive his jailers after twenty-three years of imprisonment. It simply comes down to choice, commitment to the journey, and evolution of the soul. This journey takes courage.

Lives lived in the light are powerful, purposeful, healing, and hopeful. There are countless variations to this theme, but the outcomes always involve spiritual growth and lessons learned. On the other hand, lives lived in relative darkness are lives full of negativity, fear, and hopelessness. Lessons can be learned during these lives, but more commonly the negativity that grows and multiplies stays within the cellular memory of the individual soul. This oppressive energy becomes very difficult for the soul to move beyond without the intervention of spiritual guidance and soul healing.

There is hope for everyone, but it always comes down to free will and choice. At the point of physical death, the soul of the person travels back home, where life between lives is very real. Opportunities exist on this level for healing, retraining, guidance, and rest. It is in this loving, supportive environment that souls immersed in negative energy are counselled. However, the universal rules of law and order and justice are constantly in play, and each soul must be accountable for actions that have hurt others. Planning wisely for the next incarnation can help reduce the intensity of the lessons if, through the experience, the soul is gaining knowledge, compassion, and humility.

The Garden of Eden supports all forms of life; it can and does absorb negative energy. In planning our lives, we take many things into consideration, and our commitment to maintaining a healthy earth home should always be on our list. Therefore, it is important to try to minimise a high input of negative energy by planning a life that is based in love and learning.

It is essential that we become aware and accountable for our thoughts, words, and actions. We must carefully plan our lifetimes with the best outcomes in mind. In planning each lifetime, the soul is counselled by higher beings, in accordance with the lessons it needs to learn or actions that it must account for. The soul must make amends in whatever way necessary for past actions that contributed to negative energy being laid down within the matrix of Planet Earth. This may have happened either through causing pain to another human being or causing grievous harm to Mother Earth herself.

If you live your life sending negative thoughts to others, you will download these life experiences at the time of death and move onto a healing level for as long as is necessary for you to realise the gravity of the situation and find the reasons why you acted this way. Then you must decide the best way to rectify the situation and make it up to the individual or individuals. Where many souls are involved in difficult circumstances that require amendments, it becomes extremely important to work with the justice council in planning your next life.

The justice council exists in the realm of Archangel Michael. This is the universal realm of law and order, balance and equilibrium, right and wrong. The justice council consists of enlightened beings who oversee the planning of our life contracts.

Under the guidance of the justice council, we are directed to be reborn into new lives that support our intentions to learn about humanity and bring balance to our soul accounts. Our creator does not punish us. Our creator is all-loving and certainly not vengeful. It is up to us as individuals to follow the advice of the council and set out a sacred contract that is for the highest good of all.

From a positive standpoint, those of us who treat each other with genuine kindness, acceptance, and respect will benefit from this energy being returned in one lifetime. How we feel towards ourselves is projected to others. If we disrespect ourselves and wallow in self-pity, this is what we will project to our fellow man—and this is what bounces back to us. The way we feel towards ourselves is paramount to the way we feel towards others and how we will be treated in return.

The process of becoming self-aware is a journey of self-knowledge and of introspection. All it requires is a commitment and a willingness to change for the better. Fear is an integral part of our psyches, and this is the energy that keeps us within our comfort zone of non-change. The unwillingness to change springs from the fear of the unknown, fear of taking full responsibility for self, fear of persecution, and fear of incrimination. Choosing to leave our comfort zones regardless of what is discovered takes enormous courage and strength.

The journey within is a very personal process. Every one of us is extremely complex and unique. We arrive on this planet with expectations and dreams. We come with a myriad of past-life experiences, lessons for learning, and sacred contracts. Fortunately, we also come with gifts, talents, abilities, and wisdom inherent in our souls!

The journey within takes us back to our authentic selves, back to the persons we were meant to be. The degree of difficulty comes with the level of commitment to the soul journey. Here we can lighten our loads by taking accountability for past actions that have injured or caused pain to others. We have the opportunity on this journey of life to share unconditional love with others and to connect to our truths. Once connected to our truths, we will rediscover our true purpose, our passion, and our joy.

4

I am the master of my fate; I am the captain of my soul.

WILLIAM ERNEST HENLEY
(1849–1903, ENGLISH POET)

The Circle of Life

Before we move ahead on the journey to the authentic self, we must take some time to look back and understand from whence we came. We need to acknowledge that we are each a soul living within a body of energy and light, and this body is the current vehicle in which the soul is traveling. I like to think of myself carrying the baton for my soul. Nelson Mandela was inspired by the poem "Invictus" during his incarceration. The line in this poem that I particularly love and that stands out to me as real and true is "I am the captain of my soul." We are the courageous beings currently running the gauntlet and doing the best we can with limited awareness and understanding. Here we stand, holding the baton of light, running a race we need to win.

The journey of each soul began eons ago. Each life we embark on is planned and prepared for and hopefully well lived. A life that is satisfying is well lived. A life that is full of love is well lived; a life that allows the heart to grow is well lived. A life that enjoys service to others is well lived.

Each time we enter this physical dimension, Planet Earth, we enter back into the cycle of reincarnation, and we carry with us a courageous plan. This plan is our sacred contract. We are contracted to our souls as well as to the Divine Creator, our soulmates, and soul families. The need to heal our souls plays a big part in our choices with regards to relationships, so we make plans to sort things out, make amends, close doors, help each other, and learn and love along the way.

We come to earth with our soul families, who are of similar vibration. We come back repeatedly with loved ones, family, and friends. These soul groups are very large and are underpinned by the energy of unconditional love. Our sacred contracts are extremely complex, and we are always in need of advice and guidance before finalising our plans for life. Even our adversaries come with us to help us learn and grow in love. Each soul will endeavour to love others, care about others, and have compassion for others. If we move through life's difficult lessons with grace and humility, we will be assured of winning the race as *captains of our souls*.

Someone very dear to me has recently overcome a difficult destiny link with a soulmate. This person has created an almost impossible situation for my friend to live in. Yet by the use of healing and prayer, as well as meditation fuelled with faith, the situation has been overcome. My friend has been released from a very debilitating and difficult contract. Both souls are now free of each other, and healing will take place for the adversary. My friend, who has worked diligently with light and love over many years, will be blessed eternally for her efforts.

These two women have been in lifetime after lifetime together. My friend has been victimised, tortured, and even murdered by her adversary in past lives. Yet through the power of love and faith, she has healed the relationship forever. Now the contract is finished, lessons have been learned, and the relationship has been brought back to balance for both souls. Next time these two souls incarnate together, they will not be entwined by negativity, fear, control, and torment. They will meet under new and more positive circumstances.

In contrast to this example, many families come together lifetime after lifetime to support each other's journeys and make things as easy as possible for each other. The roles and relationships may change, but the level of love and commitment to each other stays strong.

When we deal with a particular lesson and learn to accept our lives, we do not need to repeat the lessons. However, as souls, it is part of our inherent purpose to experience all that life on earth has to offer. We plan big plans, and we need the loving support of our soulmates to help us along the path.

Past life experiences impact our soul memories. Much of what we encounter on this earth is directly related to these memories and the need to clear negativity from them. If lessons planned for past lives are not learned, then they will form energy blockages for us to deal with in the present. If, for example, you need to learn about forgiveness and trust, the plans you make will support these issues and help you learn what it is you need to know.

Once a lesson is learned, it stays with our soul energy forever. It can be brought forward into the present as a gift, inner wisdom, a talent, or a positive personality trait. At this time in the evolutionary cycle of earth, we are choosing to learn as much as we can about being human. It is very reassuring to experience the wonderful benefits of our own kindness and generosity coming back to us. It is not necessary to wait for the next incarnation to enjoy these blessings.

Simply remember this: when you treat others with genuine kindness, acceptance, and respect, you will be blessed with this positive energy coming back to you. Gratitude is an important way of acknowledging your positive life choices and blessings. Reflect on your life and give thanks for everything you are happy about. Your gratitude will increase the loving vibration within your heart.

As we leave our bodies at the time of death, we once again become spiritual beings, the lightness of being that we are most familiar with. The next stage of our journey is back to our higher selves; we disengage from earth's vibration and dispose of the dense energy that held us there. We are connected to our higher selves by etheric cords that hold us securely as we live our lives on earth. At the point of death, when our souls leave our physical bodies and world, this etheric cord assists us in returning to our higher selves. In spirit form, we travel to the healing levels and reunite with our guides and angelic healers.

It is in this loving and supportive energy that we truly release and examine the life just lived. All that is tagged for learning will be assessed, and healing of physical illnesses and accidents will take place. We will be guided to evaluate this most recent journey and come to understand what we achieved, how we dealt with lessons, and what blessings we have brought home.

In my healing practice, I have on many occasions been visited by the past loved ones of my clients. It is usually through the request of the client but not always. I work closely with my higher self, so I will always check if the visitation is appropriate for the client first and foremost. When approval is given, I ask that the loved one come through with guidance and assistance. It is interesting how these visits vary. Some souls are strong and talkative; others are quiet and reticent. Others seek forgiveness, while many stand quietly, with an outpouring of unconditional love.

These visits offer the loved one who has passed on an opportunity to settle personal issues within the energy of healing and love. This is especially true when words of love have remained unspoken and when forgiveness has been sought. One father in particular comes forward frequently during his daughter's healing sessions, standing beside her in love and support. He offers comfort, guidance, and the love she is needing since his death.

One of my clients talked recently about her grandfather who had passed. She had nursed him in his last months in his home. The fact that she is a nurse helped, especially when he became very ill. My client was very close to her grandfather and was missing him in her life. His absence was bringing up deep emotions for her at this time, because her grandmother's health was also failing.

With permission, "Pop" came into my healing room, sat on the comfortable chair, and proceeded to tell me how fascinating my work was! He also told me that his granddaughter, my client, "would be very good at this." His information allowed us to uncover within her soul energy two relevant past lives. The first life that came forward was that of a medieval healing woman who was familiar with herbs and potions. The second life was that of a Chinese herbalist working in the royal court of an emperor.

The possibility of this Western-trained nurse combining past-life wisdom and current-life experiences to become a holistic practitioner in this life is very real. This form of healing interests her greatly; it has opened a new pathway and purpose for her. Pop's visit had proved very helpful as well as emotionally healing for my client.

Death is a transformation from one energetic form to another. The physical vehicle no longer supports the spiritual energy of the soul, and at the time of death, the spirit moves onto the higher astral planes. Our loved ones remain close, if needed, for a time but ultimately are extraordinarily happy to be back "home."

On another occasion I was working with a Jewish woman. She was grieving the death of her late husband. Although it had been over a year since his passing, she was struggling with sadness and depression. He had been a deeply religious man and had been the strong patriarchal presence in the family. He had been a well-loved and respected leader in his community and was missed by many. Judith was expecting him to contact her after his death with a sign that he was okay. She prayed every night, asking him not to leave her.

During her session it became apparent that Judith's husband was caught in the lower astral layers of earth, unable to move to the realms of healing and light. He had been determined not to leave his loved ones, and he consequently became stuck in this lower dimension.

Even though this was explained to him, he refused to leave his wife. Her grief and his devotion to family interrupted the normal process of death and crossing over into the light. During the session we were able to release him from the earth plane with angelic assistance, and he moved up to a healing level, which was the right place for him to be.

Judith was extremely sad but also understood that her husband needed to move on for his highest good. As the energy in the room shifted into light and love, Judith felt a release and was able to let go of the emotional burdens she was carrying.

When I saw Judith again, she was brighter and more positive. She had become involved again in her own community. The passage at the time of death to the higher realms can be interfered with through the emotions of people. Thus it is always important to pray your loved ones into the light with godspeed.

Many years ago, I was meditating on my soul's journey. My curiosity was piqued after I uncovered a life that wasn't so *nice*. I saw myself, during the French Revolution, being caught up in a maelstrom of violence, anger, and murder. I saw that I had been imprisoned for political reasons. I had spoken out against the aristocracy and been arrested for my antigovernment views. My time in prison made me angrier and more anxious. Being caught up with the negativity of the prison conditions increased my negative feelings and emotions.

I asked my higher self what it meant to now be a light worker and healer, and yet I saw a clear vision of a life of anger and violence.

The answer to this question was another vision. I saw a long line of Chinese lanterns hanging along an alleyway that went forever. Each of the lanterns held a different glow of light. There were hundreds of them! The line of lanterns demonstrated to me my past lives through linear time. Some lanterns were shining brightly, while others were dim and low. There did not seem to be any order or sense in which lantern came first.

What I came to understand was that in each life we carry the light of our creator, and the determination of how much light we bring with us is ours in the planning. Sometimes we bring in large elements of our soul energy, with lots of light and love. While other lifetimes, maybe the more courageous ones, we bring less light and love. My trail of lanterns indicated to me that although many of my lives had been well lit, some had been miserable and difficult.

I died at the hands of another prisoner during a violent revolution, because I refused to take up a weapon. My life was cut short at an early age. I was killed by someone I thought I *knew*. My desire to see change, balance, and equality for the people during this time was genuine and hopeful but maybe naïve. My imprisonment was the unfortunate outcome of my personal philosophy, and so was an early death.

I have meditated on and processed this past life, and I have gotten to know this young man. We understand each other, and I have grown in love for myself because of this experience. He demonstrated courage and conviction during those unsettled political times. With every life in which we learn to love and forgive, we can move closer to our higher self-energy.

We must trust that, during our journeys of self-awareness and introspection, we will not uncover something we are unable to deal with along the way.

I still have strong feelings about justice, equality, freedom of speech, and the right to choose. Many of these feelings and belief patterns are embedded in my soul and were experienced first-hand during my life as a young Frenchman in the eighteenth century.

My lanterns hang along the alleyway, stretching off into the distance. Each one of them represents a life I have lived, loved, accepted and, sometimes, endured.

5

When you change the way you look at things,
the things you look at change.

————

WAYNE DYER
(1940–2015. AMERICAN PHILOSOPHER AND SELF-HELP AUTHOR)

Karma is a construct, man-made in fact, that has allowed for the self-imposed enforcement of rules associated with reward and punishment. I am not saying it doesn't exist. It is just that life on earth is all about learning, and to be truly human we must experience all aspects of life. Through our actions we activate consequences. This is how we learn.

————

JOHN

The Karmic Construct: Bursting the Karma Bubble

Traditionally, karma is seen as part of the sacred contract you brought into this life. It is the accumulative energy of actions, words, and deeds, stored in your chakra system, brought forward from past lives.

In fact, it is viewed as your sacred responsibility and brings with it the need for learning, experiencing, and growing in love for self.

While you are in body, your thoughts, words, and actions will continue to accumulate and add to the lessons required for soul learning. This in turn will bring you back into life after life, until your soul journey has achieved the levels of self-love required for you to return to the source of all light and love.

Karma as a concept originates from Eastern religion; it is a Sanskrit word meaning "action, effect, fate."

This theory of karma states that whatever you put energetically into the universe will find its way back to you over time. I have reflected on this concept, and on many levels I have found cause to question it. Karma is justified in Eastern theory to support the caste system of societies and explain why some people are poor and others are not. However, does the science of physics prove this theory to be correct? The New Age movement has adopted this theory as the foundation of all spiritual growth. We have accepted, without question, this belief system.

I believe that our life is a series of lessons that need to be learned within a community of soul families and groups. The intention must always be to assist with the overall growth in love and light on Planet Earth.

I feel the phrase "what goes around comes around" needs to be reviewed under the karmic premise that energy always returns to its source. Does a car engine generate energy to run? Yes. But does this energy when generated eventually return to the car engine? No. Where does this energy go?

Does the energy of the sun return to its source, the sun? Does volcanic activity generate energy that returns to its source? To the volcano?

So why does this karmic energy theory relate solely to the human energy condition? Even animals do not get involved. Their world relates entirely on consequences of behaviour, actions, and instinctual learning.

Granted, we as humans function with emotion and free will. This separates us out from the animal kingdom, and as earlier stated, we must take responsibility for our emotions and protect our earthly home from negativity. Thus, if anger is channelled from one person to another, where does it end up? Does it automatically flow back to the sender? If joy is expressed, where does it end up? This energy flow is constant between humans, and from my experience as an energetic healer I see the projected anger being stored in the receiver's body, not returned to its source.

For humanity to answer to a supreme being that doles out reward and punishment, we have accepted karma *as a convenient concept* that will perpetuate the negative experiences of the disempowered soul and maintain the external control of an all-powerful deity. Alternatively, we could exist as wise and responsible people, living out our lives according to our sacred contracts and planned lessons. We would be accountable for our own actions and levels of joy and success.

In most societies, we have been raised on a diet of positive reward and negative punishment in the form of discipline, and the modification of behaviour within community norms. We have been programmed to expect reward for a good deed and, likewise, we would expect punishment for a bad deed. This program fosters dishonesty, lies, and manipulation. *Karma* as a concept fits perfectly into this paradigm. We monitor our behaviours with the expectation of getting the good karma ticket on our way out. Insincerity replaces genuine kindness.

There are people among us who are dishonest, takers and liars and cheats, who do not have a conscience, and who don't care about right and wrong. Yet they still can climb corporate ladders and live in beautiful homes, take holiday after holiday, go to the football, play golf at the weekends, etc. etc.! They could be described as having "good karma".

When you are focused on reward and punishment, you externalise the provider who then holds all the power. Does *God* reward us, or can we in fact simply reward ourselves? Depending on how you go about it, life can be anything you want it to be.

Living in luxury can have its obvious rewards. But is it enough? Creating a beautiful existence here on earth through the energy of hard work, accountability, kindness, caring, sincerity, generosity, honesty and love will be more fulfilling for the soul and more healing for the world around us.

Alternatively, we can live in a world of illness, unhappiness, hatred, and complaints when we settle for or choose to live in negativity and darkness. It doesn't matter how beautiful your home is, how expensive your car is, or how beautiful you are if, when you walk into your home, you are not happy on the inside.

I believe that good karma is about being accountable for all your thoughts, words, and deeds—if not in this life, then in the next. Accountability is key, as is responsibility. I would prefer that we embrace the concepts of good fortune and learning for life, because through this window we are fully in charge and can create a future that is in harmony with light and love.

We have all known people who land on their feet, live seemingly happy lives, but are not kind, generous, or caring. How do these people sail through? How are they so well provided for with the excellent job, good-looking partner, or great house? It is the temptation to follow their examples that we must be mindful of.

First and foremost, we must evaluate what is truly worthwhile and what is sold to us as a *must-have* consumerism. People who are manipulative, dishonest, who step on and hurt others, often get exactly what they want. Yet at what cost to their soul journey?

Other people are genuinely good, caring, and kind, yet still end up at the end of the queue, waiting for someone to notice them, give them a hand up or simply smile in their direction. Being a good person should be the blessing in itself. But is goodness truly valued in our societies of competition and no parking spaces?

I meet good and gracious people all the time, many of whom struggle with finances, relationships, and well-being. I believe they struggle not because they have *bad karma*; they struggle due to lack of self-worth and self-love.

The world we create should reflect kindness and generosity—for the sake of simply being kind and not for the expectation of a God-given award of merit. Expecting this reward for action lessens the action, undermining the intention. This should be called *self-serve karma*—manipulating behaviours in order to get a good karmic outcome.

I believe the word *karma* is now heavily contaminated and misunderstood as well as misused by people who feel superior and all-knowing. A comment like "She'll get her karma" is similar to ill-wishing and even cursing, using the universally accepted concept of law and order to justify being a spiritual vigilante!

I have even heard the saying "I hope she gets hit by the karma bus" or "The karma bus will take him out"!

Spiritual people are getting it wrong. The concept of karma has become a New Age construct that gives people the power to judge others, while in the meantime feeling sorry for themselves.

I believe we need to equate karma with lessons. It's simple. We all need to learn how to be human, how to be responsible and accountable for our actions, and how to move higher on the awareness scale—through unconditional love and acceptance of ourselves and others. We need to think and reflect before our actions hurt others.

Sick children are not born sick because of bad karma. A highly evolved soul may choose to come into a body to experience disease, to assist scientific research and learning for parents and humanity. Ugliness does not equal bad karma; poverty does not equal bad karma. Being sexually abused as a child does not mean you were a paedophile in a past life. This is not how it works. Being beautiful and wealthy does not automatically mean good karma. We choose our contract in consultation with beings of light, who guide us towards the best and most productive lessons for our souls in a given lifetime. Believe it or not, we have planned for and chosen most of what happens—the good and the bad.

I understand that energy is not destroyed; it can move from one form to another. With the assistance of the light beings, we can transmute negative energy into positive energy, and we can assist in the healing of our planet. As we smile and engage in genuine acts of kindness, we are adding to the levels of light on Planet Earth. As a response to these actions, we live our lives in a more harmonious world. This should be what we hope for, not to achieve elevated levels of karma/rewards so we can live more prosperous and glamorous lives. Beautiful, powerful, and wealthy people have their struggles. This is something I know to be true. I have met quite a few.

As we raise the vibration of earth through our loving thoughts, words, and actions, we are healing this planet for all of us. The Divine Creator and the universal energy of law and order will sort out the riff-raff. Murderers, predators, and thieves will meet themselves in a mirror of woe when they pass into the next realm of existence. We create our own heaven and hell; there is no vengeful God who is waiting to punish and destroy. We must all account for bad and negative actions as we complete a life cycle, but equally, we can feel assured that the goodness we have injected into the world will take root and seed hope for generations to come.

Karma is the energy of action, balance, fairness, and accountability. In the halls of justice and learning, none of us gets off the hook; every one of us must be accountable for our entire existence on earth. We should not do nice things for people in a way calculated to improve our karma. We should be kind and generous by nature and share unconditionally the love in our hearts.

Think about your soul's imprint on Planet Earth. Do not judge yourself. Just observe. If you have had difficult days or relationships, the pathway through contains grace and humility. Self-forgiveness is the key to a life well lived. The more you open your heart to yourself, the more love flows down from the Creator through your higher self. This is when *you* allow for the blessings on your path—when love of self draws them in.

Self-loathing and negative self-belief will block your path to joy. Thus you should love every aspect of yourself, despite what you have habitually believed. Let the good fortune, good luck, and good opportunities flow in from the light of Christ and our Creator. As you raise your self-love, your self-worth will increase as well. Then what you deserve and what you love will come easily to you, under grace. You are divine, and you exist in the divine order of things. Let karma be a concept that is obsolete; replace it with the choice to be accountable, responsible, and loving.

When Jesus said, "You reap what you sow," I believe he was talking about being accountable for your actions and accepting the consequence of your behaviour. In other words, if you harm a fellow human, you will need to learn what that feels like. Herein lie your lessons.

I asked John for an example. He told me about the soldier who became desensitised to death and killing over his lifetime. In planning for his next life, he chose to be an undertaker so that he could see death first-hand and, furthermore, so he could witness and have compassion for the families of the dead. This man learned how to respect the physical bodies as well as the souls of the dead, so he could offer unconditional love and support to their families.

We plan our life contracts so that we can learn what it is like to be truly human; we make choices that cover all of humanity's experiences.

We need to know what joy is. We need to know sorrow, we need to understand pain, and we need to suffer illness. We need to understand work ethic, how to keep house, how to be a mum or a dad, what kindness is, what caring is, and what it feels like to be neglected. We need to know how it feels to be loved and nurtured. We need to be creative, innovative, strategic, and hopeful. Being human is an enormous task. You have chosen this, as have I.

Karma is a poor excuse for having a tough time or a difficult life. When we reap what we sow, through enterprise, dreams, hard work, and goodness, we create a satisfying and rewarding life. We reward ourselves in the Creator's garden with abundance and joy.

It is time to re-evaluate the concept of karma and use the words "lessons and accountability." The hall of justice is where we go at the end of each life to download our life experiences. It is here we review the good and the bad, the achievements and the failures. It is here we decide our own fate through conscious appraisal of our thoughts, words, and actions. "Was I kind? Was I caring? Was I selfish? Was I thoughtful? Did I contribute in positive ways to the lives of others? Did I hurt people? Did I cause pain and suffering to others?"

In the hall of justice, we will have as much time as we need to reflect on our lives and the way they have enhanced the journeys of our souls (or how ill-conceived actions have caused setbacks). Our journeys through this earth school are not easy. However, with the help of our dedicated spirit guides and higher selves, they can become love-filled lives of purpose, ease, and joy. This is our inherent right. This is the divine plan.

6

Nothing in life is to be feared, it is only to be understood.
Now is the time to understand more, so that we fear less.

MARIE CURIE
(1867–1934. POLISH SCIENTIST AWARDED
THE NOBEL PRIZE FOR SCIENCE)

Eliminating Fear

Fear is the most disabling emotion of all. It underlies anger, greed, hatred, jealously, aggression, disappointment, and more. The process of becoming self-aware and loving is a journey through fear. Fear is an integral part of the human psyche, and it is often fear that blocks our path. The unwillingness to change comes from fear of the unknown.

The state of our world is at a critical point. The tide is turning to the light, and with the efforts of the light workers, spirit guides, and loving beings from other dimensions, the future of this planet is assured. However, we cannot afford to become complacent. There are dark forces working against us, and as hard as we try to maintain the delicate balance between light and dark, we will always be challenged.

It has become important for individuals to stand up and join the army of light workers who are busy educating, healing, and guiding others to lives based on higher values—lives based on spiritual knowledge, ancient wisdom, and present sensibility. At each stage in life people need to respond to their environment and circumstances the best way they know how. It is my intention to help create within individuals the ability to make the right choices for their personal good. Positive choices that reflect the love of self will become the foundation for positive, loving change across the whole of humanity.

Making choices is often very stressful and confusing; deciding on which way to turn or which path to take can be extremely difficult. But with guidance, it will become easier to move forward on the path of Christ light and love. Personal, daily choices will bring you closer to peace.

Your spirit guide is here to make this possible.

As a member of the human race, Jesus lived his life through his connection to spirit. He remained aligned with his higher power and was able to live an authentic, whole life because of this. Jesus was a fully conscious spiritual being living as a man. His early life was a journey of education, supported by loving and trustworthy family and friends. His mission and purpose on earth was to educate, heal, and guide. Throughout his life, Jesus maintained his sense of humanity. He lived a relatively normal life and shared it with loved ones and spiritual companions.

Jesus taught about truth, trust, faith, and love. Yet he was unable to shift the people of his time away from fear. His legacy to humanity ironically became a church based on fear: fear of God, fear of punishment, fear of women, and fear of individualised power. The negative forces that preyed on the disenfranchised, uneducated, and misguided thwarted his true purpose.

This pattern still underpins our society and culture to this day. It is still the sick, the uneducated, and the disenfranchised who are prey to the negative forces that plague this planet. Jesus made it his life's work to educate the people about their spiritual source, the God force within their hearts. He attempted to remove fear of God and replace it with love of self.

Jesus opened the way for the Creator's source of light and consciousness to be grounded in this earth during his lifetime and at the time of his ultimate sacrifice. The purity of his spirit and the light of the Creator exists in each of us at a soul level; it is up to each person to realise this and bring this energy forward into daily life.

Jesus came into body and functioned on earth as a human being, but he did not lose his divine connection to the universe beyond the veil, as we did at birth. Jesus maintained the universal flow of creator energy within his earthly body. He came for a specific purpose and carried out all that was required of him without question. He was fully informed and a co-creator of his life.

Jesus was broadly educated within the ministries of faith and wisdom here on earth. However, he wished instead for people to explore their own spirituality—with the realisation that they were spiritual beings living temporarily in physical bodies. He emphasised the way that, with each successful lesson and learning experience, individuals embrace more and more of their spiritual selves, until eventually returning home with a marvellous story to tell.

Jesus also taught about the sacredness of male and female balance. This balance is another essential ingredient to life on earth. In order to find a peaceful heart, one needs to acknowledge all of God's creations equally. Women must stand beside men as equal and complete. However, during ancient and modern history, there were few religions and civilisations that revered the female as our Creator and Jesus intended.

As women were aligned with Mother Nature, they were often blamed for floods, disease, and misfortune. When things went badly, it was most convenient to blame them. Over time, superstitions based on fear changed the way the female species was regarded. It became impossible for women to maintain their equal standing on any issue. They became lesser beings, creatures to be feared.

Since the writings of the Old Testament, when Eve tempted Adam in the Garden of Eden, women have had a case to answer. Then, along came Mary Magdalene, who was represented as a repentant prostitute in the gospels. On top of this, Mary Mother was revered because of the virgin birth of Jesus. These biblical writings set women up for failure. The sacredness of the female energy has been maligned for centuries. Only virgins held value; virginity became a trophy and a prize. The rape and torture of women as weapons of war is still as common now as in our ancient past.

Female energy makes our world go around. The woman co-creates life and then offers sustenance, nurture, and support. The male energy co-creates life but then also needs to be also sustained, nurtured, and supported. The masculine paradigm of many cultures around the world allows for the man to build on the sacred feminine base and then use this energy as a platform. The world will be a much better place when male and female energy work in total balance and harmony, standing alongside each other and mutually supporting creation and life.

Today there exists an army of light workers all over this planet, who bring in an unlimited flow of Christ light. As male and female conscious beings, choosing change, we can become an energetic entity, linking together and working for the highest good of humanity. Ultimately we will bring this planet out of darkness and into the light for eternity.

"A small body of determined spirits fired by an unquenchable faith in their mission can alter the course of history" (Mahatma Gandhi, 1869–1948, activist for the Indian Independence movement).

Each soul in this Garden of Eden has a choice, on a subconscious level, to move forward into the light or stay in the negative vibrations that allow us to resist change and continue to wallow in self-hatred and loathing. It becomes easier for many souls to stay just the way they are. The challenge to move forward is too great and too threatening. This attitude serves the darkness; it would have us all wallowing in self-pity, confusion, conflict, and hatred.

Fear presents itself in many ways. There is fear of knowing ourselves, fear of our sacred contracts and truth, fear of persecution, and fear of being let down, disappointed, abandoned, or rejected. When we as courageous souls move through the dark shadows of the past, the realisation comes that fear is a self-created illusion, entirely man-made. This powerful negative energy is created by the negative thoughts and feelings, of ourselves and others, which have become embedded in our subconscious minds. The fear holds on until the light enters and the negativity is released.

As we walk this land in this new millennium, our ancient ancestors walk with us. They exist within our DNA, our genealogy, and therefore our energetic matrix. Primal fear still defines the nature of humanity on many levels. It is therefore imperative that we understand what makes us divine.

History tells a story of the survival of the fittest, of aggression and war. The existence of this cellular memory continues to fuel our fears, our insecurities, and our stability as a global village. Tribal wars break out today as they did thousands of years ago.

Neighbourhood battles over the back fence continue. Gangs of youths fighting in suburban and city streets upset the peace. State versus state, country versus country, religion versus religion, these conflicts are still occurring every day. Conflicts such as these are fuelled by fear of lack. Disempowerment of a group denotes less abundance, less freedom, less autonomy, and fewer resources. Fear of lack is about missing out. It governs and drives many tribal and contemporary conflicts, worldwide.

The insidious battle for power, resources, ownership, and control rages day and night. This fight is fear based and rests at the root of all the negative alignment the world is suffering from at this time. Whenever an individual is threatened by a hostile takeover, the normal and accepted response is to fight. The initial reason for the takeover is the need to seize control and ownership of known resources.

There is a need to shift this fear-based action into the light. The souls of all humans need to know that all we truly need lies within our connection to the Divine. Unfortunately, greed, jealously, and lust for power tie into the battle for control, and they block the journey to divine love. If, through healing and light, we can shift this fear-based need to overpower and take from another on an individual basis, then it is may be possible to shift it entirely from the human psyche.

Part 2

Finding Your Lost Self

7

You must be the change you wish to see in the world.
———
MAHATMA GANDHI

The Journey to Love

The way in is well lit. It becomes a matter of choice whether to go there. As people learn about the world around them, they take on a higher perspective, which in its most altruistic form allows for nonjudgement and compassion. So it goes: when a people learn more about themselves, they can reserve judgement on themselves and open to self-love, forgiveness, and self-acceptance.

There is hope for everyone, but it comes down to free will and choice. At the point of physical death, when the soul travels back home, the opportunity exists for healing, retraining, guidance, and rest. It is in this loving, supportive environment that souls immersed in negative energy are counselled.

Planning wisely for the next incarnation can help reduce the intensity of the struggle. Through the life experience, the soul gains knowledge, compassion, and humility.

During my senior years at school, we were visited by priests and nuns, who talked to us about the vocation of service to Christ and God. I always felt compelled towards a life of prayer, solitude, and service. The life of a nun promised me a teaching career as well service to my faith. It was very attractive to me at that young and impressionable age.

What stopped me, then, was that I was living my life as a normal teenager and enjoying those inherent freedoms. My friends and I spent most weekends at the beach, and although I saw being a nun as a virtuous choice, I decided it was too limiting and restrictive.

However, my desire to serve and know God stayed within my heart. At that time in my life, I thought that to truly serve God I needed to be an aesthetic, a holy person, a cloistered nun or monk. Now I see how wrong I was. We can all serve the God force within us and be in service to the light, just by loving ourselves and striving for enlightenment and knowledge.

We can be married or not married, male or female, young or old, straight or gay. We do not need to be tied to any religious order or community to find the light within ourselves and be able to share it. This I know now without any doubt. I once believed that to serve God meant I would have to relinquish the opportunity to travel, to have a family and children. That belief was completely unfounded. We can have it all, if we choose.

As we begin our inward journey to self-love, fear can come and go. This is when courage and commitment are truly necessary. Eventually it becomes clear that fear is created; it is an illusion and can be conquered. When fear is released, the individual experiences a sense of unimagined freedom and joy. This is the state of grace we should all be striving for—away from fear-based decisions and choices into grace-filled experiences of happiness and joy.

The journey within is a very personal process. We are all extremely complex and unique. We each arrive on this planet with an enormous number of expectations and dreams. As mentioned earlier, the package is perfect—complex, but perfect!

In infancy, we resonate with our authentic selves, the people we are planning and meant to be. For many weeks we stay connected to the energy and love of our higher selves, but over time, as we adjust to the energy field of earth and disconnect from the divine part of our being. With this disconnection, we assimilate into the atmosphere of the world we have entered.

We are attached to the auric field of our mothers initially, but over time we create our individual energy fields, separate from theirs. As small infants, we exist for a short time in both the spiritual and physical dimensions. We systematically adjust our frequency so that we can become comfortable in the density of Planet Earth. During this time, our innate intelligence and spiritual connection work to ground our souls into bodies for further lifetime adventures.

Before this new adventure begins, we make many plans and contracts on the other side. Our souls are guided and counselled towards choosing appropriate parents, siblings, places of birth, and so on, in order to accommodate maximum learning and spiritual growth. We choose our bodies, our dates of birth, and even our astrological signs. We choose whether to be male or female. We choose our future partners, friends, adversaries, and teachers, making sacred contracts with these individuals for very good reasons.

All our choices before each incarnation are made in a fully conscious state, supported by the Divine Creator and our loved ones. It is the intention of our souls to use every life effectively. We choose many lessons, some easy and some more difficult. These lessons can range from something like learning patience to learning about racial tolerance. With each life, we aim to experience all that there is, and in doing so, we contribute to universal knowledge and information. This stored knowledge belongs to the universal mind and can be accessed by humanity for its own evolution.

Each individual soul is on a personal evolutionary path. As a baby is born and infancy progresses, the true journey begins. The energetic makeup of the child absorbs the energy that surrounds it. This includes the thoughts, feelings, and emotions of both parents, siblings, and extended family. Even before birth, the soul is fully conscious of the family it is joining. The energy transfer is effective, and layer by layer the child becomes part of its new reality.

Patterns of negative thought can begin in infancy, taken on by the child and stored in the subconscious mind. Depending on the conditions and loving qualities within the home, a child will blossom and bloom or will struggle for light. Children are energetically open to the influences around them; they do not develop conscious filters until around the age of seven or eight. This simply means that they believe whatever they hear, especially about themselves. In this reality, it becomes very possible to lay down many layers of negative and self-limiting beliefs.

Love is an energy, an actual vibration that stands alone in this universe. When love is transferred to a child they stay attuned to their authentic self. They are accepted for who they are. The authentic self needs validation, acceptance, and love to stay aligned in the light. The task of all parents is to support the authentic nature and energy of the child with unconditional love. Unfortunately, this is difficult, because every parent has his or her own personal story, and their stories define who they are and how they feel about themselves.

It is these feelings that override all good intentions and create circumstances that dishonour the child in their arms and their own inner child. This framework allows us to withhold judgement and blame. It is impossible for us to know every detail of the unwritten story of the people we share our lives with.

I believe that most of us are doing the best we can with a limited range of knowledge and experience. In every given moment, I believe, we all act in our own best interest—that is, we think we are doing the right thing. However, self-sabotage and self-sacrifice can still arise from the negative, self-limiting belief patterns we hold within our subconscious minds. So, if we self-sabotage, we still think at the moment of choosing that we are doing the right thing. The choices arise from our subconscious belief patterns. And they seem right— even if these belief patterns are born from fear!

The degree of difficulty on our journey of introspection comes with the level of commitment to the journeys of the soul. Here we have the opportunities to lighten our load, share unconditional love around, and connect to our truth.

The concept that love is a noun is often new to people. Love is a thing, an energy; it is specific and real. As simply a word, it is easily used and misused. It is a word that can ring very hollow but also a word that can carry true meaning and energy. Love is the name given to the vibration of unconditional acceptance, nurture, and joy that emanates from the God force, the Creator, the source of all that is. This energy is healing, supportive, and all-powerful in its essence. It can be consciously channelled to others as well as withheld. Without love from our Creator, we would perish.

Love vibrates within the whole body, giving life and energy to every cell of our being. It is centred in the heart chakras and resonates at the vibration of pink and green. Pink is the vibration of spiritual love, while green is love manifested in the physical dimension of our bodies. It is actual; it is real. It is not just a word. When love is perceived as a real energy, it can be directed where it is most needed and used for the highest good. It can be directed into our own hearts as well as into the hearts of others.

The conscious channelling of love raises our individual vibrations and reconnects them to the source. Our spirit guides can access this love portal on our behalf, and when this energy is channelled into our physical bodies, it brings with it the miracle of spiritual, emotional, and physical healing. When love is channelled into the life force of an infant child, the baby thrives, sleeps peacefully, grows, and is happy. Infants starved of love in this physical world suffer immensely. Love is an essential part of our human condition; we need love to grow our spirits and our hearts and our bodies.

My husband and I left Sydney with our four young children in 1991, with the intention of building a childcare centre in the South Coast area of New South Wales. After investigating the possibility of buying an existing centre in Sydney, I was struck one day with the idea of heading out of Sydney to fulfil this dream. At the time, I was driving through afternoon traffic with my youngest child in the car, going across Sydney to pick up my two oldest children from primary school and number three from preschool.

I just knew that leaving Sydney was the right thing to do. I now call these inspirations *downloads* from my higher self. My husband agreed it was a promising idea, and so we set about making plans to sell up our Sydney home and move south. We saw the South Coast as a wonderful place to raise our own family and build a new and enjoyable life for all of us. On top of that, the fishing and the beaches are incredible!

The philosophy behind our childcare centre was based on creating a safe and secure haven for every child that walked through our door. Having four children of my own and being a primary-trained schoolteacher, I saw the absolute necessity for early education within a stimulating and nurturing environment. Our staff were employed because of their genuine love and respect for children and their understanding that each child was unique and special.

We often commented on how easy it was to identify a child that came to us from a loving home, a home of stability, nurture, and care. Some parents and guardians could drop off their little ones with ease, without fuss, while other children would be anxious, unsettled, and unhappy.

Love is an energy that settles the child within an environment of trust and security. Children who were loved shone like bright stars; their eyes were shining and their smiles endearing. Unfortunately, there were children over the years who didn't smile, who were not well cared for and obviously emotionally neglected.

Love is aligned with light. There are degrees of light, as there are degrees of love. The truth, however, is that as long as light exists in a space and time, darkness fades away. In a similar way, the essence of love will always raise the vibration of a place, person, or circumstance. As with light in a darkened room, love can change perceptions, outcomes, relationships, and situations. While these neglected children were in our care, they were loved, nurtured, safe, and well. This is what we offered them for the entire time they spent with us. I know it made a difference.

Sharing Love

Here is a worthwhile and practical exercise to do.

Sit in a comfortable place and breathe yourself into a relaxed state of awareness. Now picture in your mind something that makes you smile, makes you feel wonderful, makes you feel connected to spirit.

Thinks of some thing or person that you truly love.

Bring your focus to your heart centre by placing your hand on your heart. Now imagine a bright-green light shining there.

Visualise the object, person, or circumstance you began with showered with a soft, shining green light. Connect the object, person, or circumstance with the light at your heart. Feel the connection strengthen as you focus an intention of love.

Now see this light envelop you, and breathe this light gently in and out. Consciously project this feeling of well-being and happiness to something or somebody you love. Feel the energy flow through you; enjoy this experience of sharing love in this physical world. You have made a difference! When you have finished, give thanks to the source of love.

Do this simple exercise daily, and you will notice a difference in your energy and feelings of well-being and happiness. It is also possible to improve relationships when you use this technique.

8

Knowing yourself is the beginning of all wisdom.

ARISTOTLE
(383 TO 322BCE, GREEK PHILOSOPHER)

Knowledge is power.

SIR FRANCIS BACON
(1561–1626, ENGLISH PHILOSOPHER AND SCIENTIST)

The Way in Is Well Lit

If we desire to raise the light levels within our own beings, we need to venture within and uncover the lost and unloved parts of our selves. By going within, under the guidance of spirit, we can learn about our purpose, our spiritual connections, and our role in the divine plan of our lives. This inner knowledge and understanding opens the door to personal love and self-acceptance.

It also becomes possible to clear emotional blockages that are holding us in negative thought patterns detrimental to our spiritual growth.

Negative thought patterns are supported by belief patterns taken on through childhood experiences as well as during past lives. During the early childhood years, we are energetically open—unfiltered—so very able to take on many layers of negative patterning that completely define the adults we become.

It is important to remember before embarking on a journey of healing and forgiveness that many of our soulmates and loved ones are endeavouring to step forward on the same journey. We have come together in soul groups in this spiritual school to help each other through our lessons and sacred contracts. However, once we arrive, we become unconscious beings and simply forget about our well-made plans.

We forget about the contracts we have signed with our parents, brothers, sisters, partners, and friends. It is only through the journey of introspection and healing that we can once again become aware of the entire picture. From this heightened state of awareness, we can move into compassion, acceptance, and nonjudgement of others as well as ourselves.

The goal for all of us, therefore, becomes one of healing the whole self. With this intention, we assist in the healing of the planet. We are all connected under one divine umbrella; through this divine connection we can assist humanity's evolution at the same time as we heal ourselves.

Our creator holds a dual identity, which is reflected in the nature of men and women. Through this duality, our Garden of Eden continues to exist, procreate, and grow. As we contemplate Mother Earth and Father Sky, we align ourselves with our true nature. While we live and breathe on this planet, we are carried in the arms of our Creator Mother, and as we look to the sky, we are enlightened by the ancient light and love of the Father.

The destiny of all of humanity is linked to this planet. As individuals, we have the responsibility to support the physical world through our spiritual development. The higher the vibration within each of us the higher the vibration on the planet. Mother Earth supports us unconditionally, so in turn we must be willing to support her energetically as well as physically.

Once a soul chooses to make a difference within, help moves forward. Spirit guides align, and the person is guided towards healers, books, teachers, and music—whatever is required. Mother Earth is truly one of the most sacred healers, and at our doorstep she stands. Simply by tuning in to the warmth of the sunlight or the cool, refreshing waters of the beach, river, or lake, the soul is nourished and supported.

Taking a walk through the forest or park will raise our awareness of the abundance that is provided for us. Again, we can take note of the green! How truly beautiful our planet is. All the colours of nature reflect our own energy systems; we are deeply connected to this planet. This is our Garden of Eden.

The fact that we are so closely aligned with Mother Earth gives us more food for thought when we embrace a path of healing. We have at our fingertips an enormous range of healing medicines, herbal remedies, and healing modalities.

Over thousands of years, crystals, minerals, and plants have been used to heal the physical, emotional, mental, and spiritual energies of humanity. All that we have is part of the divine intelligence and the divine plan. We are truly supported in this realm, and it is up to us to educate ourselves and understand the vast resources Mother Earth holds in her hands to help us.

In my practice, I align my energy with my higher self and work on bringing light and love into the client for healing. I was never really aligned with crystals and minerals, but over time they aligned with me! After buying a few, I quickly added to my collection and studied the properties of each crystal in conjunction with my understanding and my healing practice. It wasn't long before crystals became my friends and an integral part of my entire life.

I feel the connection with the divine intelligence within the crystal, and I invoke this intelligence through my higher self to work in harmony and healing for each client. Through my practice, many people over the years have opened their hearts and minds to crystal healing. Children in particular are naturally connected to and attracted to crystals.

I remember a time when my healing practice on the South Coast was opened to the public during school holidays. A family came in with a young boy about eight years of age. He had fifteen dollars pocket money to spend, and he insisted on buying a collection of "rocks." His mother thought otherwise! She insisted that he keep his money for the specialty lolly shop down the road. I stayed well out of the cross-fire, as the little boy convinced his mother he didn't want lollies—he wanted "rocks"! After some serious haggling, this very happy customer left my shop with a beautiful collection of crystals in a pouch, ready to join the other "rocks" he had at home.

It is very rare that a child will leave my practice without a crystal firmly tucked into his or her hand. Children have innate senses that adults have often buried. As we look at the children in our lives, we see the true essence of authentic selves that are pure, good, and whole. Ultimately, our journey through healing to unconditional love of self will lead us back to our own love-filled authentic selves. These love-filled selves are what many happy children demonstrate day by day but what many adults have lost.

As you step onto a path of spiritual growth and healing, you may be drawn to certain crystals, aromatherapy oils, herbal essences, or even food. Follow your inner guidance and your gut feelings; choose in every moment to be a better person. Your world will change for the better on many levels—for you, your loved ones, and the people in your circle of influence.

MEETING YOUR SPIRIT GUIDE

9

The two most important days of your life are the day
you were born and the day you find out why.

MARK TWAIN

Enlisting Help from Our Spirit Guides

The love of our creator is limitless. We are part of creation, and we exist within it. Each one of us is connected to the others through our connection to our ultimate source. Our soul energy is fuelled by love, and it will always exist. When we feel the need to re-enter life on earth to take up our journey again, we do so with the utmost care and preparation.

Each soul exists within its higher self-energy while on the other side. When we venture into earth's dimension, we leave this heavenly home, and we leave our higher power. However, we are not alone. We travel with many other souls who share sacred contracts with us, and we are also part of large soul families and groups. As we choose to reincarnate, we enlist the counsel of loved ones, guides, and others.

At no time are we left to fend for ourselves and make soul-changing decisions on our own.

Our dearest loved ones and soulmates usually work alongside us, making plans of their own, so we can support each other. Contracts are drawn up regarding accounts, agendas, responsibilities, and lessons. All the circumstances of life are considered and planned for.

The element of destiny is also a significant part of our grand plan. Contracts are written between certain souls to advance the journey of both. However, the destiny link does not always come to fruition if other random energies and circumstances take a soul off their path. In the planning stages, two souls may choose to marry, when and if other contract clauses are sorted before they meet. If circumstances are not completely ripe for the marriage, the two souls may never cross paths.

Each of us has a grand plan, a sacred contract supported by our higher selves and our souls. This contract is designed to bring us back to perfection as we grow our hearts here on Planet Earth, in our Garden of Eden. The detail in our contract can be randomly affected by life's misadventures and unplanned experiences, so staying as close to the grand plan as possible makes for a life well-lived, purposeful, and pleasing. A satisfying life is a worthwhile goal for any intrepid earth walker, especially considering the density of the energy and the random elements of life in this dimension.

To assist each of us in staying as close to our grand plan as possible, we have enlisted spiritual help. The problem is that as *unconscious beings* we are not aware that this help is available to us. From the time of our infancy, we become disconnected from our spiritual family and home. The familiar environment from whence we recently descended becomes locked in our subconscious memory.

Children can be aware of a certain *presence* in their lives and for many years communicate with this presence telepathically, but usually this

55

communication eventually becomes blocked. Children have been known to entertain imaginary friends; these nonphysical beings are often the child's loved ones or guides.

I clearly remember a night when my eldest daughter was about three and a half years old, when she called me into her bedroom. She pointed to a space behind me and asked me, "Who is that man?" I turned and could not see anyone, of course. When I asked her what he looked like, she said he was all white and shining and smiling at her. My daughter smiled back to this loving being, showing an open and loving acceptance of her spirit guide. She had no fear; her innocence and trust connected her then to her guidance in love.

Guardian angels have long been spoken of as loving beings watching over our children, but we also all have spirit guides, who are totally dedicated to our well-being and life-purpose. Spirit guides are angelic in nature but belong within the cycle of reincarnation. They have lived lives on earth, processing their lessons, growing their hearts, and evolving into beings able to guide and assist others.

Realms of angels also exist and are dedicated to the well-being of humanity. Angels do not normally incarnate, and if they do, it is for a specific purpose. They do not engage in the cycle of reincarnation. Angelic beings exist for us on many levels; they support life on earth as messengers, protectors, guides, and healers.

Angels are aligned with all elements of Mother Earth as well as with all elements of human nature. They are here to support our earthly existence and make our lives as easy and blessed as possible.

Spirit guides, on the other hand, have been chosen by us in counsel with enlightened beings. They assist our entry into this physical dimension at birth, in conjunction with angelic alignment, and they stay with us until we journey back home. Our spirit guides are loving and trusted friends. We know them well, and they have journeyed to earth with us before, sharing physical lifetimes and experiences.

We knew them in a past life as loved ones, trusted colleagues, mentors, best friends, or even husbands or wives, brothers or sisters. Our connection to them is deep and loving. They have stepped forward to watch over us, nudge us, and guide us towards the best possible outcomes in every moment of our lives.

We chose our spirit guides before birth. They stand as our master guides and will do whatever is in their power to do. They cannot override our free will and choice, but when it comes to making choices, they will assist to support the changes that we wish to embrace. Our spirit guides will filter thoughts through, provide opportunities, and strengthen our intuition and gut feelings so that we act with confidence and assuredness in any given moment.

Our spirit guides also filter our higher self-energy, which allows us to bring more light into our lives, and with this light, energy and love from the Creator. Our spirit guides love us unconditionally and know us better than we know ourselves. They stand alongside us at birth and are never far away. The more light we welcome into our lives, the more positive our energy and the more our spirit guides can do. However, when we become fully conscious of their presence and dedication, we can benefit even more.

Communication is the key, and regular conversations with our spirit guides will strengthen our connection here on earth. Communication can be in the form of requests for help and guidance during meditation, prayer, or quiet reflection. We should always remember to be quiet in the moment so messages from the spirit guides can reach us.

It is important to take the first step in getting to know our spirit guides. Every morning as we put our feet on the floor, we can say good morning to our spirit guides. We can welcome them into our day and ask them to make the day as easy as possible. They will do all in their power to make our days shine. They just need to be asked.

Here are some examples of spirit guide stories.

In the following stories, the names of the people and the names of their guides have been changed.

Hans and Janine

Hans lived in Northern Europe. He was the father of a large family, and he ran a dairy farm. Noel was his eldest son.

As the eldest boy, Noel was expected to stay on the farm and live his life out as a dairy farmer, eventually taking over from his father. However, Noel was extremely intelligent and very well read; he had always intended on studying at university. When Noel left quietly one day at age fifteen, Hans, his father, gave him his blessing but was extremely sad to see him go. He knew he might never see him again. As they said goodbye, Hans promised to pray for him and always keep him in his heart.

Hans was regretful for not showing Noel his love and affection during their life together. He has now come back as a spirit guide to Janine, offering complete protection and guidance as well as unconditional love for her in her current life. Noel made his way through to university and became a professor of theology, studying creationist theories and Darwinism. He was dedicated to his work, but as it happened, he neglected his own family emotionally. It was necessary for Janine to resolve that issue in this life by dedicating herself to her family as a mother and wife before embarking on a career path as a counsellor and teacher.

Peter and Anne

Peter is Anne's spirit guide. Anne was a woman living in a beautiful, but wild, Irish coastal fishing village during the early 1800s. Her husband was Peter.

Peter and Anne had a large family, five children in all. In that past life, Anne was a loving and devoted wife, mother, and community leader. She had a strong personality and was always the first one to put up her hand to help other villagers when times were tough. Peter was not home a lot; he was often away fishing in dangerous waters, making a living to keep his family well nourished and cared for.

Anne worried about him and prayed daily to the holy mother to keep him safe. She kept a simple but beautiful altar in the window and kept a candle burning for Peter. Their love was strong and good. However, during a stormy night, Peter lost his life at sea. Anne stayed up all night waiting for him to return. Her instincts were strong, and she feared the worse.

When he didn't return, she was devastated. Anne questioned her faith and her purpose. How was she to raise her family without the man she loved and relied upon?

Peter is here now with Anne, as her loving and devoted spirit guide. In this life, she has planned to reignite her faith in the divine and raise her energetic vibration both spiritually and emotionally. When Peter came through for Anne, he told us that as her guide he will never leave her side and that his love is eternal. He is here to help her have the best life she can possibly have, whatever she chooses to do!

Black Feather and Claire

Black Feather is Claire's spirit guide, and they have travelled together in many lifetimes as soulmates. Black Feather is a highly evolved soul. He has aligned in this life with Claire to help her bring forward her natural healing abilities. Through her ancestral line, Claire has inherited psychic ability and the power to heal. These gifts have been passed on from generation to generation, and now Claire stands as the guiding light for her entire family. However, because of personal circumstances, these abilities have been buried under an energy of low self-worth since childhood. Claire was the medicine man and healer for her tribe in a past life, and Black Feather was her son and student. Now he has the opportunity to repay in kind the loving mentoring and guiding support Claire offered him.

The time has now come for Claire to deeply honour and value herself, bringing herself into the spotlight. It has been customary for her to sit at the bottom of the list, the last rung on the ladder. It is no longer appropriate for Claire to live her life in the shadows, and Black feather will help guide Claire to be the best person she can be!

Martin and Andrew

Martin is Andrew's spirit guide, and again, these souls have shared many lifetimes together. The one that best represents their strong relationship was in nineteenth-century India. Both men served in the army during the time of colonial rule. Andrew was a master strategist and planner. He assisted with the rail network and infrastructure for the entire Indian subcontinent. Andrew was struck by the levels of injustice and hypocrisy within this society, and he worked closely with the indigenous men and women in building a network of travel that enhanced their lifestyle and economy.

Andrew appreciated the sense of order the British were bringing to India, and he firmly believed in his heart that they were there to help improve the situation. Martin was Andrew's brother in that life, and he always held an optimistic view of every situation, whereas Andrew often felt frustrated and thwarted. Both men were intelligent, religious, and good-hearted. At all times their intentions were for the highest good, and yet they battled in every direction to make a difference.

Now Martin is with Andrew to help keep him in a positive frame of mind, especially when Andrew gets overwhelmed with the frustrations of daily life. Andrew has been living with Parkinson's disease for twenty-three years. At times he is overwhelmed by his lack of power and autonomy, and he still feels strongly about injustice and hypocrisy in our world. Martin is here to help Andrew view the world through the eyes of spirit and to bring hope and joy to Andrew as he embraces his spirituality, personal development, and healing.

Dana and Jacob

Dana is Jacob's spirit guide. Jacob was an Allied soldier during World War II. He was shot down in Italy and rescued from a field by an Italian family, who healed his wounds and kept him safe. As he healed, he repaid their kindness by looking out for the family's well-being. Jacob loves to cook in this life and could cook from an early age. He is good with flavours and understands food. This culinary connection has come from his time in this warm and hospitable Italian family home during the 1940s. Dana was the eldest daughter, and she spent hours teaching him to cook. Their relationship was based on a great friendship and lots of fun. Jacob's heart, however, was already taken! He was in love with a Jewish girl who had been taken prisoner by the Nazis. Jacob's time in Italy with this family was well spent and very enjoyable but unfortunately short-lived. Jacob eventually was healed from his wounds and returned to his troops, only to die in battle a few months later. Dana is with him now, in a loving and supportive way, guiding him and protecting him from danger. She guides him within the energy of sisterly friendship and unconditional love.

Wallis and Susan

"A life lived well is a life that satisfies the heart, body, and soul" (John).

Susan emailed me for a reading in 2008. She was struggling at the time with a young family and a busy husband. Susan was feeling disconnected from the outside world due to her responsibility to her family, but also because she was missing her work and the purpose this had given her in the past.

These words were for Susan.

"Your Spirit guide stands beside you and has done since the day you were born. His name is Wallis. He is honoured to be back with you, assisting your journey into the light. The life you lived together was during the British Empire's expansion by sea into the New World. Again you are moving into a new world, and he is here to help guide your way through the darkness. In your past life with Wallis, he was the captain of one of the queen's ships. You were his second in command and on one occasion saved his life after a sailor attempted to gather forces for mutiny.

"Your name in this life was Charles, and you were a man of intelligence, courage, integrity, and honour. Wallis is offering you his love and devotion, as you so bravely dedicated your life to his. At this time you bring into this world the same gifts to humanity. Your soul energy is advanced, and your ability to understand and process the nonphysical world is beyond most. Many of your earthly experiences have been unusual and difficult to explain. However, by now connecting directly to Wallis in meditation, you will really begin to make sense of it.

Your current life is relevant in many ways to your life as Charles, and the parallels are blessings to draw on. With the guidance of Wallis, you will learn more and more about yourself, and it will all make perfect sense.

Susan, the most *obvious* path ahead is the one you must take. There are paths that will take you away from your truth and paths that will run parallel but will keep you off track. Working closely with Wallis will assist you to make the right decisions with regard to your career. Consider what skills it takes to be a maritime officer, and apply the skills to what you already know.

Consider courage, wisdom, vision, organisation and planning, supporting others, coordination of the whole, and planning for the greater good. All of these traits are inherent in you. They will be drawn on at different times of your life and in the future will be the basis of your journey. Many of these traits will assist with the challenges of parenting; many will assist with the challenges of work and career."

Amy and Julie: A reading from John

Amy is Julie's spirit guide.

"Julie, you and your spirit guide have shared a lifetime together. This is always the case, and your guide could be a relative from a past life, a friend, a parent, or a sibling. Whatever your relationship, you can be assured it was one of love, respect, and mutual caring. That is why Amy is with you and has always been by your side. This world is too dark and difficult to come here alone and unguided. Our creator has provided us with the perfect solution, a loving companion in spirit who will look over us each day.

Julie, let us begin by explaining the life you shared with your guide. You were sisters in America during the Civil War. You lived in North Carolina and were the daughters of a plantation owner. Your sister's name was Amy, and your name was Barbara. At a young age both of you were sent away to school, and you became very close and protective of each other. Amy was older and took her role of big sister very seriously. The years were turbulent, but in the safety of the college, you grew into fine young women. This was a pleasant life for both of you, with not too many restrictions.

Your parents were loving and supportive and wished for both of you to experience the best that life could bring. Because of your education, you returned home with a broad outlook, and both of you supported and respected the emancipation of the slaves. This attitude brought unwanted attention to you both at times, but you stood firm and became very respected women in your community.

The traits that kept Barbara in high regard still sit within your soul energy, Julie, and can be drawn on at any time. You have a big heart and see the underdog as needing support. Remember that not all battles can be won, but it is always worth having a good try, especially when injustice is prevalent. Your sense of righteousness is something to be proud of. You know when something is wrong, but more importantly, you know when there is something you can fix.

At this time of your life, your sense of helping and caring has been overshadowed by a desperation to keep your head above water and to keep your business alive and well. The fun that you should be having is also being overshadowed by the same stress. Amy and you always made time for fun and games, laughter, and enjoyment. Julie, you must make your way back to the energy of light and love. Amy can help you, once you know what to ask for and how to ask."

This next story is a little different!

Maya and Meredith

Meredith came to me for a healing session. Relationships were proving difficult for her to maintain, and she was still a single woman. During her first session, her beautiful Polynesian guide stepped forward. This spirit guide's name was Maya. Maya's energy was supportive and incredibly gentle, wise as well as feminine. My client was hoping for something more profound, and she dismissed the whole concept of spirit guides. This did not bother me, but I felt concerned for Maya, as she was being rejected. As it turned out, Meredith came back for many sessions, and Maya would always be present, smiling and gentle. She was not bothered at all by Meredith's feelings and attitudes. Maya came from a place of pure devotion and unconditional love.

Over time we established that Meredith lived life as a seafarer and had met Maya and her people as she explored the islands of the Pacific. Meredith's name was Christos. With his crew, he came across a community of islanders who openly accepted them into their village life for a time of rest and replenishment. Christos fell in love with Maya, but due to her cultural and spiritual beliefs, they could not be together. Unfortunately, this relationship was doomed, and they parted ways with broken hearts.

The unconscious memory of this heartbreak was the reason why Meredith could not open up to the love and guidance being offered by Maya. However, over time and with deep heart healing, Meredith came to accept the presence of Maya into her life. Meredith's gratitude increased, and the relationship became one of loving support and guidance. It is interesting when gender roles change from life to life. It is important to understand that the love on offer from our spirit guides is never a romantic love. The love they offer is purely divine in its source.

Linda and Justine

During World War II, Justine lived a life as a soldier named Sam. As it turned out, Sam was injured in a blast and lost his vision. On returning home to England, he recovered in a rehabilitation hospital, where he met Linda. She nursed him and cared for him and eventually fell in love with the cantankerous soldier called Sam. Linda introduced Sam to reading with Braille, and over time they became deeply involved.

Linda even took Sam for rides on country roads on the back of her motorbike, just so he could feel the exhilaration of speed and fresh air. He learned to trust her deeply, holding on tight and enjoying their day trips.

Now Linda stands with Sam as Justine's spirit guide. In this life, Justine works in the field of optometry, helping people of all ages to see better. What a gift to the world!

Justine's favourite poem as a young child was "The Soldier" by Rupert Brooke. She was never sure why she loved this poem so much, because it was so far removed from her current life. She knew it word for word and often recited it.

Since Justine has connected with her spirit guide, Linda, she now understands why—her past life as the soldier named Sam who was wounded in the war explains it. His nurse, Linda, who loved him so much, came back into Justine's life now as her spirit guide. Justine is an optometrist and loves helping people with their eyesight.

In a more recent healing session we saw that Sam had travelled in the North Sea around Scandinavia before being injured on board his vessel. This vision was validated when it was discovered via the internet that the British army had been stationed in Iceland during World War II. Justine has had a burning desire to travel to Norway and Iceland for many months now. She has finally booked her ticket to visit this unique and beautiful part of our world.

Richard and Esther

Esther came into my healing practice many years ago with a severe fear of drowning. During her first session, we introduced her spirit guide, Richard.

The past life Richard and Esther shared was one of brothers living in far North America. Esther was called Peter, and he was the youngest member of a very happy rural family. The first vision I saw of Peter was on a raft-style boat with his dog; they were quickly being swept into the middle of the lake that was at the back of their farming property. He was heading to a small island in the middle of the lake, and the message "The grass is greener" came into my mind.

I could see Richard standing on the bank waving to Peter, wishing him well. However, Peter's dog panicked and fell into the water. Peter drowned before he reached the island, while trying to save his dog. Richard did not realise this had happened, as he had turned back towards the house.

We worked with this initial information and spent time healing Peter's traumas with the loving help of Richard, in spirit. Esther was able to release her fear of swimming and drowning.

However, Esther recently came in for another healing session; she spoke about feeling blocked in her third-eye chakra. During the session we were guided back to Esther's past life with David. The story unfolded. Richard and Peter's family were under attack by savage invaders. Fires had been lit around the house, and the rest of the family had been isolated and trapped. Richard had risked his life to get Peter to the boat for safety, but unfortunately, everyone in this family died.

Peter had been told not to look back, just to look at the island, and everything would be OK! Peter did look back. He saw the house on fire, and he knew in his heart that all was lost. That was when his energy system shut down, and through fate and destiny, he also died.

Richard is with Esther now, as an all-loving and protective guide. Richard has promised to ensure Esther's safety throughout this life as well as offering her guidance and love.

No matter how traumatic a past life might be, it can be healed with conscious awareness, understanding and love.

Our spirit guides stand with us in nonjudgement. They understand the difficulties of our journeys, and they know all about our contracts and more about us than we'll ever know! That is why they can help; that is why they are here. Our spirit guides supports us, in the epitome of unconditional love. They offer us this love and protection whether we are consciously aware of it or not. The guidance they offer is fuelled by love, and they will do all that they can, in all ways possible, to assist us in our life plans.

Often it has come to pass that in previous lives our spirit guides were unable to help in the way or to the extent that they wished. Such was the case with David and Peter. This fervour and love spurs them on to do all that they can this time around. Maybe we helped and loved them equally, so now they have their chance to return the favour.

Whatever the circumstances, we know that this these are friends indeed, spiritual friends who we can rely on and call on at any time. Spirit guides are themselves highly evolved beings. After many incarnations they have reached an elevated level of spiritual growth, which gives them the option of learning through spirit-guide work rather than by continuing the cycle of reincarnation on earth. Spirit guides exist in a realm of their own; they are well trained and attend spirit guide school before being qualified to take up the position. Souls on target to raise their spiritual awareness while incarnating on earth will always bring with them a spirit guide with the experience to assist.

Our spirit guides will open spiritual doorways for us; they just need to be asked. Meditation is an effective tool for connecting with our guides, but simply having the desire to make contact can also bring them closer. Above all, trust is essential. We need to know that we have chosen and contracted with another loving being to help us get on track and stay there.

We begin each life with our spirit guides supporting us. When we are children, our spirit guides are very close by, with their arms spread around us. As we grow up and need to learn and experience life, our guides move back, but not away. When we are adults, they stand by us, but they cannot override our free will, so in many circumstances they are unable to intervene or help. Therefore, when asked, our spirit guides are filled with joy at the prospect of being able to help.

In addition to being our protectors and guides, spirit guides filter our higher-self-energy and become the conduit of spiritual awareness, love, and wisdom that is contained within our higher selves. As individuals learn lessons, heal, and grow, the vibration of the physical body is increased, which allows for more higher-self-energy to flow down.

In the correct order of light, the spirit guides facilitate spiritual growth and ensure that the will, purpose, and dedication of all individuals are supported in unconditional love. Our journey here in this Garden of Eden has been undertaken to experience all there is to know about the human condition. It is our innate capacity to offer compassion, empathy, and love that will ultimately fuel our journeys home.

It is also through life's varied and challenging experiences that our hearts are enabled to open to ourselves and others. Opening our hearts and endeavouring to keep them open is one of the greatest challenges.

10

I have reserved my potential until now. So that we can walk in
the light safely, establishing a quiet light revolution together.

JOHN

Light Will Protect

*You are about to begin your own
journey of introspection and healing.*

As you make changes to your routines and embrace the valuable
benefits of meditation, it becomes necessary to raise your awareness
regarding energetic protection. On a spiritual and energetic level,
there are all kinds of challenges that you have to face as you choose
to change the paradigm of your life. As you move into the higher
realms of spirit and light, you can call on your spirit guides to help
keep your energy topped up and balanced in the simplest of ways.

Human beings interact with one another on many levels. Etheric cords
connect us and allow the transfer of information and energy. These
cords can be so strong they can hook into your physical body, keeping

you connected to people permanently, without your knowledge. You can feel the emotions of others when hooked into their emotional bodies. Or you may not be able to get someone out of your thoughts for days after talking to them. This is because of the cords.

The cords work both ways. This means that you will be corded into people as they are corded into you. By removing these cords, you will free up the energy between you and the other person.

The etheric cords can easily be removed with the assistance of your spirit guide. Occasionally, after talking to someone, you may walk away with a headache or even feelings of nausea. This will occur if the person's energy is dense, dark, or negative.

I have met clients in my healing practice who have suffered from migraine pain for years. When they remove the cords in their third eye and crown, the headaches stop occurring. Even some chronic pain can easily be alleviated with the removal of stubborn cords and hooks.

Areas of vulnerability are the forehead and temple, the heart, the neck, and the lower back. There is always a reason behind the hook-ins, and with awareness and healing it is possible to find out the underlying cause. But in the meantime, it is most effective to ask your spirit guide to help.

Protecting our energy fields is easy to do, and we do it because we value our lives and our journeys. It is not done with fear; it is done with self-worth! Our energy fields are precious, and the time we spend improving our lives through meditation and healing is time well spent. In order to maintain our growing energy, we must clear and remove other people's energy from the auric field and chakra system, thereby protecting the spiritual work we are doing.

In New Age text, the referral to cords being cut is quite common. On reflection, I ask you to imagine a cord or hook planted firmly in your heart. If the cord was cut by your spirit guide, there would remain a section still imbedded in your energy field. The procedure we use is one of *pulling out* the cords completely in both directions and then transmuting the cords into positive healing energy for Mother Earth.

Cutting ties is another concept altogether. This happens when you consciously choose to move away from a person or group of people. The actions you would take would include taking their number out of your phone, returning their belongings, and so on. These actions are done in the physical world. However, if you wish to move these people from your energetic world, you would need to remove all of their cords from your energy system.

PEOPLES CORDS.

The following procedure is the best way to remove the etheric cords of others.

Removing Cords and Protection

At the end of each day, and when you are feeling tired or overwhelmed with other people's energy, you can use this process of removing cords to bring you back to centre and focus.

Sit down in a quiet space, making sure you are comfortable.

Take three deep breaths in through your nose and out through your mouth. Begin by visualising a column of white light all around you, and ask your spirit guide to step forward and align with you within this column of light. See this light column expand all around you.

Ask your spirit guide to remove all cords from your energy field and send them up into the column of white light. Then ask that all cords that you have sent into others also be removed from these people and placed into the column of white light. Here the cords of energy will be converted into healing energy for Mother Earth.

Now ask for your energy field be topped up, from head to toe, with a vibrant white light. You can also offer this light to those people you have corded into—*be it their free will and choice to accept it*. If others do not accept your offer of light, ask for it to be converted into healing energy for Mother Earth.

Most people welcome love and light when it is on offer to them, but on occasion this offer is rejected.

The next step brings with it protection. You are asking for protection from negative energy and harm's way. You are asking to be protected from lower dense and dark energy that is projected to you by others. Again, this procedure is simple but very effective.

Ask your spirit guide to bring down as many golden spinning hoops of protection as you need. The golden spinning hoops protect your energy from others'. You can do this several times a day simply by asking your spirit guide, "Please protect my energy field."

Become aware that you are in a column of white light, and gently the golden spinning hoops float down over your entire body, one at a time. As they float down, they create a vibrant curtain of protection that energetically deflects negativity away from you.

Your spirit guide knows what level of protection you need, so allow him or her to provide you with the appropriate number of golden spinning hoops. With practice, you will be able to adjust your own levels, especially when you know you are heading into some dense energy such as a hospital, a movie theatre, or public gathering.

It is essential also that you practise this protection procedure at the end of every meditation you do. Meditation opens your energy field in a safe and controlled way, but when you are finished, you need to be grounded and fully focused, back in your body, and ready for whatever life has in store.

Take a moment now to practise your removing cords and protection procedures.

11

Only when you are relaxed can you see what's going on.

———

JANE CAMPION
(AUSTRALIAN FILM DIRECTOR)

The Healing Path, Through Meditation

You have probably noticed that I have often referred to the term *healing*. Let us take a moment to reflect on what this word really means. To heal is to fix and make better; it means restoring, reconciling, or rebuilding. This is what we know. The process of physical healing comes to us from within the cellular structure of our bodies; we also know that our cells thrive on the pure energy of love.

We often take physical healing for granted, as it is part of our bodily functions. We assume we will get better but don't usually question how. The healing of our physical bodies happens in front of our eyes, be it a cut finger, a bruise, or a twisted ankle. Over time the body takes care of itself.

Occasionally we need to call on the help of a doctor or similar practitioner, but we know healing happens naturally most of the time. Physical healing usually is hastened when the patient is cared for by a nurturing loved one, a nurse, or a companion. The energy of love heals everything, both in the physical body as well as the emotional body. Loving thoughts, words, and actions help each one of us to get out of the sickbed and back to our daily lives.

The path to your higher power and spirituality also requires a state of well-being and health. The healing of the emotional body as well as the physical body, the mental body, and the intellect, allows for the person to fill with light and love from the source of all that is good.

Healing happens when dark or negative energy that is caught in the body is cleared and removed. Past experiences that have caused pain, heartache, or sadness will create energy blockages that stop the flow of light and love. Wherever these blockages occur, light and love cannot enter.

Taking charge of your own healing is very possible with conscious awareness and by making the decision to release pain and emotion from a past negative experience. Underlying all physical illness and disease is an emotional layer of negative beliefs, thinking, or experiences.

Simply, it becomes a matter of reflecting. "What is working in my life and what is not?"

Thoughts that exist in the mental body are responsible for your reality tomorrow and the next day. It becomes imperative that you listen to what you say *to* yourself *about* yourself, to check the flow of negativity that can create illness, unhappiness, and isolation down the road.

Again, these thoughts may not have originated from you. They may have been said about you or told to you as a child. Whatever the source of this negative thinking, it can be held within your subconscious and eventually have an impact on your well-being. These thoughts may have belonged to a parent, teacher, sibling, or lover and been told to you often enough that you came to believe them as true about you.

The journey through healing for any individual will include the healing of the thought patterns and emotions that have created the current reality. Feelings of disempowerment, futility, and hopelessness are an accumulation of years of negative thinking that now define you as an adult. If you give enough energy and attention to a thought, it can become ingrained in your belief patterns.

Belief patterns cause all sorts of trouble, especially if they are not true. The authentic self becomes buried under these untruths and blocks the way to your higher self.

Meditation is the essential tool you need to open yourself to the vast and inspiring truth that is your authentic self. Meditation becomes the key to introspection.

Meditation is the practice of creating stillness and relaxation so you can tune in to your inner voice of guidance and wisdom.

This inner voice can direct you to the areas in your life that need attention. The world is noisy, hectic, and almost impossible to quieten down. It is up to you to make the effort and enjoy the silence once again.

Meditation allows the conscious self to step aside and open to the spiritual self, thereby giving access to the spiritual realm. Within this realm the spirit guides exist, waiting with divine patience and love.

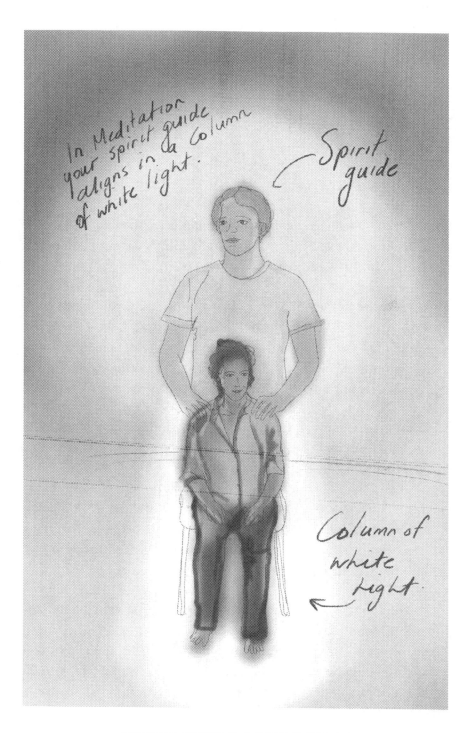

In Meditation your spirit guide aligns in a Column of white light.

Spirit guide

Column of white light.

SPIRIT GUIDE ALIGNMENT

79

Setting up Your Special Space for Meditation
Silence is the sleep that encourages wisdom.

———

SIR FRANCIS BACON

To benefit from and enjoy your meditations, it is very important to create a dedicated space within your home. This space may be in your bedroom, living room, or sunroom. Wherever it is, it needs to provide you with privacy and peace.

Furnish this space with a comfortable chair, a small table, and maybe a cushion and throw. Sitting upright will enhance your meditations, as it will help you to stay conscious and aware.

To increase the ambience of your meditation space, you might enjoy lighting a candle or burning a favourite essential oil. Crystals will also be a wonderful benefit to you while you meditate. Choosing crystals is easy: amethyst, clear quartz, hematite, or fluorite are just a few that can help you stay conscious while on your journey of awareness.

Meditation is relaxing, but it is also a conscious journey of discovery and enlightenment. Laying down or meditating in bed will often result in sleep, not meditation.

Decide on what time of day suits you best and allow yourself a minimum of thirty minutes. Sometimes it takes a couple of minutes just to sit and breathe and allow yourself to rest. Once you begin your meditation, you should be feeling calm and peaceful.

Make sure you have prepared well by turning off your phone and informing your family or housemates that you are meditating— so please do not disturb! Peace and quiet are the main keys to a successful outcome with your meditations. It is important to be comfortable and to begin by relaxing yourself through the process of gentle breathing. When you place both feet on the floor, the energy from your spiritual self will flow through your entire body and be grounded into your earth-star chakra, located below your feet. This chakra is the energy centre that anchors your spiritual self within your physical dimension.

Place your journal and pen nearby.

I recommend daily meditation practice, but if that is impossible, plan for at least three or four times a week. The more meditations you do, the higher the vibration of energy will be created within your meditation space in and around your chair. Your meditation space will begin to draw you in, because it feels so nurturing and relaxing to be there.

Meditating is not hard, but is a skill and a discipline. With practice, you will find it gets easier and easier. Some days you may feel dissatisfied with the process and other days you will be overwhelmed with insights and understanding. The secret is to persevere and enjoy the time with your spirit guide. If you are having difficulty relaxing, go back to the simple breathing technique, breathing in through your nose and gently out through your mouth.

I have introduced many people to meditation practice, and often their first response is about time restrictions. The nine-to-fivers and the stay-at-home mums are usually stressed over time. Believe it or not, even people with the biggest excuses find themselves meditating daily—some of them even twice a day!

It is all about commitment to yourself.

I have recently introduced three women with young children to meditation. Each said they would find it hard to find the time. They each began by getting up a little earlier each day, before the children. From then on, time found them. All three mums now meditate regularly, bringing wonderful benefits to themselves and their families.

Meditation is a dedication to yourself. Every time you sit in your comfortable chair you are affirming your self-worth and value to your spirit guide and your higher self.

This meditation will allow you to create the bridge between your conscious mind and your subconscious mind, allowing you to connect to spirit. *Creative visualisation* is a process that uses the power of the mind to create a new reality in which to learn about yourself. The goal of meditation is learning and self-discovery. The wonderful blessing of meditation is that it is easily done in the privacy of your home. So even when emotions come up and truths are uncovered, you are safely and securely supported in *your private space*—with the energy of unconditional love provided for you by your spirit guide.

By following the guidelines and instructions given here, you will create a wonderful, sacred space for yourself. This is the platform to your path of purpose, understanding, acceptance, and love.

Creative visualisation allows you to harness the power of your mind and your imagination to create a sacred space, your own perfect Garden of Eden. Within this garden, you then place yourself under the guidance and support of your spirit guide.

Meditation is a tool for self-reflection, awareness, and healing. The journey within is active and conscious; you must stay alert as you receive messages and build connections to your guidance. In these experiences you will be led by the hand into a new world, and by staying conscious you will return with gems of gold in the form of wisdom and guidance.

With the practice of meditation comes some other lovely surprises. An aura of peace and calm begins to build around you. Questions that have worried you are answered. Decisions are made with assuredness and ease. Your day moves easily forward, and life becomes much easier on many levels. When you request help, your spirit guide does all in his or her power to assist.

Health benefits are also very real. Stress levels can drop, and even high blood pressure is known to be aided through the practice of daily meditation. As you develop a loving and trusting relationship with your spirit guide, opportunities come your way. People and events step onto your path. Surprises happen; good things take place. Your desire for happiness, prosperity, love, and well-being are acknowledged by your guide—so just ask and trust.

The level to which you receive these blessings is relevant and aligned with your feelings of deservedness and self-worth. By building a loving relationship with your spirit guide, you build a loving relationship with yourself.

Our meditation process uses the power of the mind to create a space for your spiritual self to visit. In this space, your spirit guide is able to communicate with you. At first it may not be completely clear and you may not see what you are expecting to see. Persevere, and over time it will happen for you. Images, words, or thoughts may flash into your mind; this is just the beginning, so trust that you are on the path to success.

Your spirit guide has a name. Remember that he or she is a loved one from a past life. Ask your guide his name, and allow for it to flow into your consciousness. Trust what you hear or see, and over time the name will be validated. You will then be able to call on your spirit guide daily by the name you have been told.

Take charge of your meditative experience. Create a beautiful, sacred garden with your mind's eye, and become familiar with every corner. Pay attention to the colours, the beauty, the flowers, the trees. The potential of your private Garden of Eden is unlimited. Ensure you include a crystal-clear stream, a waterfall, and a rock pool. Pay attention to what you love the most and enjoy the entire experience.

Your journal becomes an important companion on your journey of introspection and awareness. Keeping a journal close by in your meditation space gives you the opportunity to write down your thoughts. People receive information in different ways from their guidance. Some people see visual scenes and depictions, while those with an auditory gift may hear words of encouragement, messages, or even warnings. There are, however, many more people who find it difficult to translate the messages or get clear indications of what is being channelled through. This is where your journal helps.

At the close of your meditation, open your journal and begin to write. At first your writing may consist of loosely held together words or statements, but over time a fluent dialogue will take shape, and your words will resonate with meaning and understanding. The words written in this relaxed and peaceful state will come from within and from above.

You can also use your journal to navigate a line of questioning by writing down your queries on the left-hand side of the page at the beginning of your meditation. Then, when coming out of your meditation, you will find yourself writing the answers to these questions on the right-hand side of the page.

Be patient and trusting, even when the flow of insights seems slow or blocked. There is always a reason. Something that you want to know about may be blocked on a level that is not allowing access. Be persistent and consistent. The answers you seek will come to you in perfect time and in perfect order.

I call this process "joining the dots." Over time, journal entries and ideas come together, forming a picture that gives you a deep insight or awareness. The notes in your journal of colours, pictures, words, and feelings will occasionally bring about important healing through conscious awareness of a given life experience. All the individual bits of information don't mean much, but when you pull them together into a bigger picture, they makes perfect sense. Occasionally these light-bulb moments may occur while you are driving your car or even having a shower. Once you get the realisations or answer, don't forget to give a gracious thank-you to your spirit guide.

The follow-up meditations then become a process of raising memories and feelings around the experiences that have surfaced. Your spirit guide will offer healing to you during meditation at your request and allow any negative memories and emotions to be released with love.

As your communication with your spirit guide develops, it is important to remember never to interfere with the personal issues of a friend, family member, or colleague by interfering in his or her life. Requesting information about another person in meditation can bring with it negative consequences and accountability.

Be careful what you ask about, and always hold any information you receive close to your heart. You can ask whether the request you are making about another person is ethical or appropriate. Your spirit guide will honour only the highest good, so be respectful in your enquiries.

Meditation and communication with your spirit guide is the path forward. This practice will fill you with light and inform you. Remember that regular practice will bring with it incredible results. The decision to step on this path is entirely yours.

Remember always to *protect your energy* once you have completed your meditation and journal. The golden spinning hoops will ground you and offer you the protection you require.

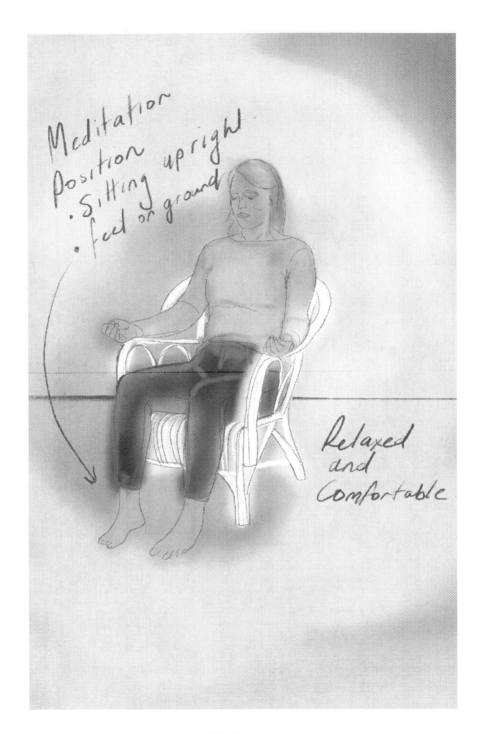

MEDITATION POSITION

Prayers of protection are included in my channelled meditations. It is important to consciously align in light and love before beginning any meditation. The prayers given here open your energies and request protection, verification, and guidance.

Dear Spirit Guide,

In the presence of light and love, I ask that I may be filled with the holy light of the universe. May this light energise and revitalise my body. I ask for help, guidance, wisdom, and teaching. I ask for my highest guidance to come through.

In the name of the divine creator of all that is, I ask that you verify this being of light to be my spirit guide who works in the light. I ask that my spirit guide step forward now and be aligned with me in the presence of light and love and in the name of the divine creator of all that is. And so be it that I work in love and light, and I work with my spirit guide, who works in love and light.

Amen

Meditation with Your Spirit Guide

As you sit in a comfortable upright position, visualise a brilliant white light shining down over you. Relax and breathe this white light in through your nose and out through your mouth. Relax more and more with each breath.

Continue with your breathing, in through your nose and out through your mouth.

As you visualise and focus on the white light, see it gently flowing over you and through you, into every cell of your body. See the column of light expand and totally surround you.

Be aware of how you feel and how relaxed you are becoming. Continue with your breathing.

The light is changing now into a vibrant green. See this green light energy flowing down over you, all the way to your feet and into the earth below. The green light is forming an energy mat at your feet.

As you continue to breathe, you feel yourself gently moving upwards within this green column of light. You are gently floating and moving into a sacred space full of light and love.

In this space you are surrounded by beautiful green grass, colourful flowers, trees, and a flowing stream. This sacred space is safe and secure and exactly how you would want it to be. Take some time building your sacred space, filling it with colour and light.

Focus on your breathing, and relax in this special place.

Your spirit guide is there waiting for you.

There is a soft shimmering lavender light ahead of you, and from within this energy your spirit guide steps forward. Your spirit guide is holding out his hand, offering you a connection of love. Take a moment to step forward and embrace this being of light.

Here in your sacred space you have been greeted by your loyal and trusted friend, your spiritual companion. Feel the loving energy being offered to you in this moment.

Now it is time to get to know this wonderful being of light. Walk ahead together and find a comfortable place to sit and talk. It may be under a tree, or beside the stream, amongst the flowers, or next to the gentle waterfall. You choose, and enjoy this time with your spirit guide.

You can ask questions of your guide or simply be open and receptive to the guidance that is offered, but importantly, you should relax in the company of your guide and be open to the loving support.

Initially the messages of help and guidance might be hard to decipher, but with patience and trust, this process will get stronger and easier.

Stay with your guide, enjoying this time together.

When you feel you are ready, embrace your spirit guide in loving gratitude as you now walk back across the vibrant green grass, back to the column of green light. Gently and slowly you will feel yourself floating back down into your body. You are now realigning your spiritual self with your physical self.

Again, take a moment to focus on your breathing.

Now ask for all the negative energy that has been released during this mediation to be collected in the green energy mat at your feet. The energy mat can now be offered up to be transmuted into positive healing energy for Mother Earth.

Give thanks to your spirit guide, and take time to write in your journal.

When you are finished, ask your spirit guide to close down your energy field with the golden spinning hoops of protection.

I am often asked whether meditating away from home is okay. Some people like to sit directly in the lap of Mother Earth, either at the beach or in a garden or park. However, meditating away from home can bring with it a few problems. We have already spoken about the creation of a safe and secure environment to meditate in, and this is extremely important for a number of reasons.

To begin with, it becomes necessary to build the energy in which to meditate effectively and easily. Also, your private meditation chair is a safe place in which to express emotions, allowing tears to flow if need be. It is where you journal your thoughts, feelings, and emotions. It is where you can completely relax.

That said, mobile meditation, away from home, is possible if you follow a few important guidelines. If in nature, like the beach, park, or garden, you need to gold-bubble yourself entirely by asking your spirit guide to assist. Visualise yourself completely encased in a bubble of golden energy all around you, even under your feet. If the area is busy, it will be more difficult to relax and focus, so your results may not be as profound as with your home meditations.

A colleague of mine was quietly meditating on a beautiful secluded beach. She was deep in meditation when a big, friendly dog bounded up to her. The dog meant no harm and was most likely attracted to the positive energy around her, but my friend was startled and shocked. She came crashing out of her sacred space and back to earth with a thump. Experiences like these can be very unnerving and upsetting, so be aware. Think about where you choose to meditate when you are away from home.

Frequently I am asked whether it is all right to meditate on your way to work by train or bus. Busy people seem to think this is the only time they have. The short answer is no! Again, remember that during your meditation you are entering a sacred space within the spiritual realm, and it is important that you respect this.

Public transport in any city is full of other people's energy. Keeping your energy clear and protected takes a huge conscious effort. So be mindful of this, and again, respect yourself in decisions you make on where to meditate. This is a very important path you are now on. Your spirit guide will help you find time to meditate, so ask for help in planning your daily schedule.

12

Following the light of the sun, we left the old world.

CHRISTOPHER COLUMBUS
(1451–1506, ITALIAN EXPLORER)

Using Light and Love to Heal

As we look around our physical world, we see many things. Within this third dimension, our sight is a valuable tool with which we decipher, observe, learn, and process all that goes on around us. Our physical bodies contain many other aspects for learning: we have the sense of smell, taste, touch, and hearing. These physical traits help us assimilate and move through this third dimension with relative ease, giving us the ability to sense danger and make decisions for our highest good.

However, there is so much more to the physical body and this physical realm. There is an invisible world of energy that moves through and around us daily. Some people are extremely sensitive to this energy, while others are oblivious to the effects it can have on us. Yet science classes in primary and high school refer frequently to energy.

Electricity is a flow of positive and negative energy. We cannot see it, but we know of its existence due to the impact it has on our lives and the help it gives us.

Danger exists within the energy of electricity, but most people do not focus on this aspect. They simply go about their daily routines, turning on the television or computer whenever they choose. Positive and negative energy exists everywhere in our world, and this energy is complex and all-encompassing. We avoid the dangers of electricity when procedures and policies are followed and strictly adhered to. In the same way, with the physical body we can avoid the danger of negative energy by following procedures and policies and by paying attention to detail.

We are an energetic body made of millions of molecules, supported by an energy source that we refer to as God or the Creator. Within each cell of our bodies we hold the God source, which is often referred to as the life force. This life force is connected to the Creator. I will show you how to connect to and bring this energy forward consciously, with guidance, to support your journey and the journey of your soul.

We live in a physical world, a three-dimensional world. We are confined within physical bodies, but through spiritual practices we can access other realms and dimensions. Our spiritual selves exist within us, and it is this connection to the divine source that we need to understand more fully.

Our bodies are energy in motion. We have seven main energy centres, called chakras. The chakra system is our personal energetic storage system, I like to refer to it as our home office! Aligned with the chakras are seven energetic astral layers, which form our auric field. These are called the astral bodies. The energetic motion we speak of exists in our cellular structure at the molecular level. Movement and action at this level is generated and sustained by the energy flow down into the chakra system from the higher self. The more open this channel, the more light travels into our bodies.

This energy flow down is our life force. It is not of this world but exists in it and allows us to exist on earth. The life force forms our spiritual selves, our souls, our connection to our higher selves. Our life force is gifted to us from the Creator. Is it eternal, it is love. When this life force is drawn away from us through the processes of illness, fatal accident, or acts of violence, our physical bodies cannot be maintained. They no longer thrive and simply cease to exist.

Our soul energy, however, is an entity unto itself. At the time of physical death, the soul disconnects from the physical body and returns to the spiritual realm for healing and processing. The physical body is the vehicle that was housing the soul, but once the vehicle is damaged beyond repair, the soul returns to its original source and home.

It is extremely important for the physical body to stay well and energised in order for the soul to carry out planned lessons and sacred contracts. It is also essential for the body to maintain good energy flow and good health. As the soul arrives, in infancy, the authentic self is fuelling the journey, but as we have talked about earlier, this precious and perfect energy begins to take on energy from this dimension even before the child is born. The authentic self becomes compromised, and negative layers begin to take shape and form.

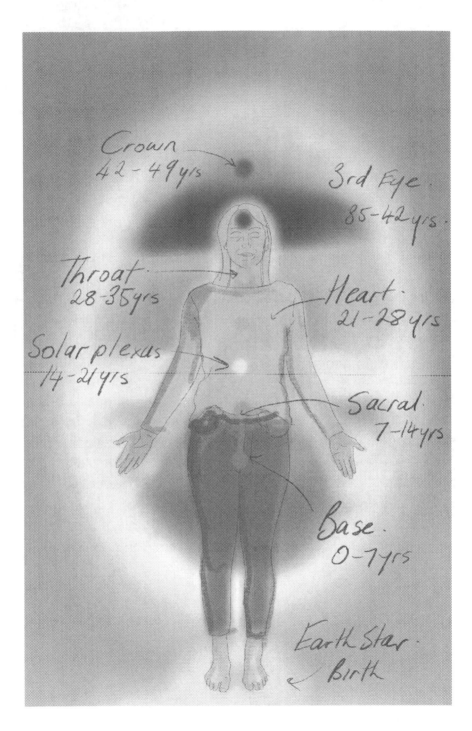

CHAKRA SYSTEM

13

You can't stop the waves, but you can learn to surf.

PROFESSOR JON KABAT-ZINN
(FOUNDER OF MINDFULNESS-BASED MEDITATIONS)

The Chakra System

The chakra system holds the layers and memories of positive as well as negative influences and energy. Everything we experience is filed away with attention to detail and in perfect order. The chakra system then becomes our pathway to spiritual growth and physical health, both of which are necessary so we can stay here in this dimension long enough to complete our sacred contracts and lessons. The chakra system is complex but very easily accessed with the help of our spirit guides. When the chakra system is accessed through meditation, healing of the soul is truly possible.

Each chakra aligns with a specific colour vibration, and when we access this colour, healing can happen at a deep and profound level. The colours resonate at the perfect vibration to suit the individual. When channelled by the spirit guide into the body, they will assist to clear and balance the energy field. Colour exists in all aspects of our world as a gift from the Creator and Mother Earth. These same colours flow through our energy field.

Let us now look at the chakra system in detail.

"There is only one corner of the universe that you can be certain of improving, and that's your own."

———

ALDOUS HUXLEY
(1894–1963, ENGLISH WRITER)

The Earth Star connects us to earth. It is the embryonic chakra that allows the soul to connect to earth, separate to the mother's energy field. This chakra centre is *white-gold* in vibration and appears as a sphere below the feet. The Earth Star can be damaged and unsteady, just as all the other energy centres can. It is imperative for the soul to be connected into the Earth Star for a healthy life to be maintained. The Earth Star holds records of depression, suicidal energy, trauma, and accidents that may threaten life. It develops during the embryonic stage, and its strength is determined by the Garden of Eden in which it grows. This chakra is our connection to earth and is aligned with the elemental energies of earth. Here we are anchored into the earth plane at the time of birth. The Earth Star records are kept in association with the duration of life itself. The Earth Star is monitored by the higher self.

The Base Chakra develops between birth and seven years of age. Events during these years are recorded in the base chakra energy centre and form the foundation of life in the physical body. The inherent need for survival and the right to exist in this time and space are defined during this period of life. The vibration of the base chakra is aligned with the *colour red*.

The base chakra is deeply connected to the energy of the mother. The quality of nurture, care, support, and love will define the child as well as the adult he or she will become. The unconditional love that is given to the young child helps seed the heart chakra. If a child is not loved, this directly compromises the ability to love self and others. If a child is loved with conditions and strings attached, he or she will also be compromised as an adult and will have difficulty accessing pure divine love accurately.

During the early childhood years children are naturally drawn to loving people and environments. They seek out love; they need it to grow. When love does not exist within the hearts of the mother and father, then the child can become needy, attention-seeking, and insecure. Behaviour problems in children relate back to the quality of light, love, and attention they receive on a consistent basis, year after year.

There are a myriad of reasons why children need medication and strict diets to manage behaviours. However, adding large doses of love and attention, time and patience to the family mix will enhance all parent-child relationships and help improve unacceptable behaviour that may have developed within the child.

Children need boundaries; they need rules, routines, and behaviour guidelines that are acceptable to both parents. These allow the child to mature in a trusting environment that they can count on and be sure of. Consistent expectations, kindness, positive attention, and time spent together will ensure a child grows up with a trusting and self-assured nature. In a perfect world, the loving home environment creates a strong and resistant base chakra as well as a potentially strong and loving heart.

A child who is loved, nurtured, and allowed to blossom will have good relationships as he or she grows older. These relationships are formed based on mother love, guidance, and trust, as well as unconditional nurture and support.

This base chakra is situated at the lower hip level. It anchors your spiritual essence to the physical world in a context that supports your reality. It connects directly to the Earth Star and is aligned with your divine right to exist.

The condition of the base chakra defines the way you live, love, and communicate in this physical world. It begins development at birth and continues for seven years. During these years you are directly tied to the energy of your mother and to survival, trust, nurture, and security. The base connects to the feelings of belonging as well as separateness and loneliness.

When your way of life is threatened, the base chakra is activated for fight or flight. A healthy base chakra creates feelings of belonging in the moment, patience, structure, and stability.

Cultural, racial, and social issues also govern how life is expressed in the base chakra. This energy centre is directly linked to ancestral and genetic issues. A healthy base allows for feelings of security, which foster tolerance and acceptance of others.

To strengthen your base chakra, create a structure around your life and home. Routines, planning, and goal-setting always strengthen the base. Create an environment that supports your physical life on all levels. Nurture and mother yourself with time out, kindness to yourself, and self-awareness.

Cultivate patience, relax, and allow things to come around in time. The base chakra is aligned with nature and Mother Earth, so spending time in nature will strengthen your base.

The Sacral Chakra develops between the ages of seven and fourteen years. Events during this time are recorded in the emotional body and define the emotional stability of the adult as well as relationships and quality of life. The value placed on self holds strong here, and this attitude towards self will define how much joy, abundance, and good health the person feels he or she deserves. The vibration of the sacral chakra is aligned with the *colour orange*.

This chakra connects directly back to the father and the quality of his relationship with the child. A loving and supportive father offers the child an enormous sense of personal value and confidence. Again, this loving energy needs to be offered unconditionally by the father for the child to access maximum quality of life.

As the sacral chakra is aligned with the emotional body, it is essential to keep it clear and flowing. Many issues settle in this chakra, creating blocks to good health and well-being. The first and foremost issues that need to be addressed here in healing are those issues concerning the relationship with the father.

Women who have difficulty finding a loving relationship can trace emotional blocks back to the way their father treated them, as well as their own perceptions of what men are like. Men who have difficulty with loving relationships can also trace their feelings of self-worth back to their relationships with their fathers.

When an individual has strong self-worth and a positive attitude towards self that is natural and easy, his life flows along smoothly, and things come to him in positive and synchronistic ways. The intention behind healing the sacral chakra is creating healthy relationships with *male energy*, and this includes employment and career. Abundance, prosperity, and well-being are aligned with our divine right to live our lives in joy and happiness. A healthy sacral chakra supports a life such as this.

Sexual energy and reproduction also sit in the sacral chakra, so it is important to clear the energy here of past relationships and ill health in order to keep the energy of reproduction healthy. The sacral chakra needs to be well balanced for the rest of the body to stay on top of things.

Many health issues originate in a blocked sacral chakra, because emotions underlie ill health. Keeping the sacral chakra full of light will empower the individual to better health and well-being and a strong sense of self-worth.

The Solar Plexus Chakra develops between the ages of fourteen and twenty-one. Years and events happening during these years define the maturity of the adult, the self-confidence, and the sense of self that one takes into one's adult life. These are very formative years, as one grows through teenage challenges into a responsible young adult. Personal power and the need to control our world sit here. The vibration of the solar plexus is aligned with the *colour yellow*.

The solar plexus is aligned with the mental body; it is here that thoughts are processed and decisions made. We understand when something feels right. This feeling sits in the solar plexus, the seat of intuition and knowing. It becomes very important as we grow older to make decisions for ourselves and choose what is right for us. When we make positive and intelligent decisions, we move to responsible adulthood. It also helps a great deal when we make these choices with a strong connection to spirit—that is, aligned with our highest good.

The base chakra is connected to the mother energy, and the sacral is connected to the father energy. The solar plexus is connected to the autonomous self. During these years of development, the individual learns about himself through friends, school, relationships, and life experiences that happen inside and outside the childhood home. The stronger the sense of self and the more positive the self-esteem a person enjoys, the easier the journey to adulthood becomes.

During the healing process, it becomes necessary to identify any negative, limiting belief patterns that have formed over the early years of childhood. These belief patterns will take hold in the sacral chakra as attitudes towards self, and they will eventually be manifested in the base chakra as your reality. What you truly believe will be what you live. The power of thought is the energy that we need to manage in positive ways for positive outcomes.

Listening to what you say about yourself, to yourself, is the secret to removing limiting belief patterns. It's like washing away the negative thoughts and replacing these thoughts with positive affirmations. Using the bright-yellow light provided for you by your spirit guide will help you shift into the positive.

The Heart Chakra develops between the ages of twenty-one and twenty-eight. It is the prime centre for the flowing down of unconditional love from your spirit guide and the higher self. This is where love flows in and out. Love is the life force of the body, both energetically and physically. Without love we do not survive. The vibration of the heart centre is aligned with the *colour green*.

The capacity of the heart to offer and receive love depends greatly on whether you were loved as an infant. If not, then it becomes essential to grow your own heart's capacity, by reseeding it with divine love and love of self. Learning to love yourself begins with self-knowledge and acceptance. This is the journey to your higher self, the journey to divine love.

When the heart chakra is open and healthy, it is easy to live a joyful life. The physical heart is essential for good health and a long life; it is incredibly important to allow love in. Sadness, grief, rejection, loss, and trauma all will close aspects of the heart chakra. When it is fully closed, physical health is compromised.

Simple daily activities such as gardening, walking in nature, singing, dancing, and meditating will promote love within the heart chakra. Opening the heart and releasing pain can sometimes be difficult, but the results are always worth the effort.

Mother Earth supports our existence here on her planet with unconditional love and acceptance. All she needs in return is respect and care. The healing she provides for us comes without judgement, and it can fill our hearts with joy. Take the time for yourself to go outside.

The Throat Chakra is a delicate and complex energy centre. It develops during the ages of twenty-eight to thirty-five. The throat chakra is aligned with personal truth, spiritual communication, as well as communication in the physical world. It envelops the throat as well as the ears, so it affects speech, hearing, and smell. The throat chakra resonates to the *colour blue*.

Emotions are expressed through the throat chakra, and blockages here can create illness. It is an important pathway to the higher self that will blossom under the energy of integrity and honesty.

Activities to strengthen the throat chakra include writing letters, writing a journal, singing, talking, and laughing with friends. Listening to beautiful music or enjoying your favourite album also strengthens this energy centre. It is important to remember that gossip and negative talking can damage the throat chakra.

Also, as the centre of free will and choice, the throat can be severely compromised by controlling relationships and dysfunctional workplaces. Being forced to do something you disagree with weakens your freedom to choose and stand up for yourself.

It is always beneficial to develop the ability to stand in your truth, to be assertive but not aggressive, and to speak from your heart.

The Brow Chakra, or Third Eye, develops between the ages of thirty-five and forty-two. This energy centre is the seat of wisdom and perception. It is where thinking and understanding are distilled into knowingness and acceptance. The third eye resonates at the vibration of *indigo*.

As inspiration or thoughts pop into your mind, they are processed according to learned behaviour, expectations, and understanding. The third eye chakra allows for the clear clarification of this knowledge and wisdom, and when aligned with your solar plexus it forms the energy on which decisions are made.

The third eye is also the doorway to the mind's eye, and many people see into the nonphysical world through the gift of clairvoyance. The third eye can be used for telepathy as well as prophecy. It must always be used with integrity and aligned with the highest good for all.

Activities to support and strengthen the third eye centre include the regular practice of meditation, study, reflection, reading of uplifting and inspiring material, and spending time with like-minded people.

The Crown Chakra is the seventh major chakra within the physical dimensions of the body. It develops between the ages of forty-two and forty-nine. It is the gateway to your higher power, the place where your spirit guide accesses your energy system. The crown chakra resonates to a *soft lavender colour*. It is situated just above your head. It is here that the flow of light and love, inspiration, and guidance move into your physical body. Your spirit guide stands there, close by, offering help. The crown chakra is supported by meditation, prayer, and stillness. Taking time out of your day to simply "be" will significantly help your crown chakra as well as your connection to your divine guidance.

Beyond the crown chakra is the "transpersonal point." This chakra opens to your higher self-energy and the wisdom of the universe. The colour here is *silver-white*. It is through this gateway that your higher self communicates with you. Your soul energy connects from the transpersonal point, all the way down through the chakra system, into the grounding and supportive energy of the earth star.

Even if you have trouble remembering things, your body and your energy system do not. To journey to your higher self-energy, you must take the path of healing. Healing happens when the chakra system is balanced, clear, and free of emotional trauma, stress, and illness. Your higher self cannot access those parts of you that are holding onto negative energy. Thus, in order to raise your vibration, it becomes essential that you open up your energies and process the blocks that often exist in the chakras.

In our next meditation, we will revisit your sacred space. This meditation aligns you with energy and light from the Creator, filtered down from your higher self-energy by your spirit guide, and into your physical body, through the chakra system.

In order to benefit from this process, it is important to allow your spirit guide access to your energy centres. You do this when you are relaxed and receptive to the help on offer, and the best time for this is during meditation.

During the chakra balance meditation, you will be guided back to your sacred space and taken to a magnificent waterfall of light, colour, and energy. As you stand under the gentle flow of light, your chakra centres will open, allowing for the release of negative energy, negative feelings, and negative emotions.

Your chakra system will be filled with light and love and brought back into balance.

WATERFALL

The Chakra Meditation

Begin with your prayers of protection (page 87).

As you sit in a comfortable upright position, bring down a brilliant white light. Let it wash over you all the way down to your feet.

Breathe in this pure and balanced energy as you relax further and further.

As you continue to breathe and relax, visualise the column of light changing to a vibrant green. This green light moves over you and through you, flowing down to your feet and forming a green energy mat.

This green light starts to expand, and a column of light forms all around you.

As you relax, you feel yourself floating up into this column of light. Be aware that you are moving into your sacred space, the sacred space you have created for yourself out of love and light.

As you enter your sacred space and step onto the vibrant green grass, you see your spirit guide waiting to meet you and assist you with this process.

You are now guided to walk along a green path of light, towards a light-filled waterfall. This waterfall is full of light, energy, and colour. It is magnificent, as it flows gently down over the crystalline rocks into the stream of cleansing water.

Step into the stream and stand under the waterfall. You can feel the revitalising energy wash over you and through you. Enjoy this experience.

Now become aware that the energy within the waterfall is changing to a soft red. See this red light move down over you, into your base chakra, and into your feet. Feel this energy cleanse and balance this energy centre, removing negative energy that is stored there. As you stand under the flow of red, breathe this energy into every cell of your body. Allow your base chakra to fill to overflowing with this red energy.

Become aware now that the colour is changing to a soft orange light, and this light is flowing over you and through you, into your sacral chakra and down through to your feet. As the orange light flows through you, it opens up your sacral chakra to allow the release of negative energy, feelings, and emotions. Continue with your breathing, as you focus on bringing the orange light into every cell of your body. See your sacral chakra fill to overflowing with this orange light. Relax and enjoy this energy flow.

Now become aware that the colour of the waterfall is changing to a soft yellow. This light flows down over you into your solar plexus and through you, all the way down to your feet. As the yellow light fills your solar plexus to overflowing, it allows for the release of negative energy, feelings, and thoughts that are stored here. Breathe in this yellow light and feel your solar plexus strengthen. Relax and enjoy this moment.

As you stand in the waterfall of colour and light, become aware that the colour is changing to a vibrant green. Focus on bringing this light into your entire being and into your heart chakra. See and feel this light flow down through every cell of your body, down to your feet. As your heart chakra fills to over flowing, it allows for the release of negative energy and emotions that are stored here. Breathe in this green light, and fill your heart and lungs with this loving energy.

Now we move onto your throat chakra as the waterfall changes to a soft-blue colour. See this blue light flow gently down over you, into your throat chakra and then though the cells of your body down to your feet. As this energy opens up your throat chakra, it allows for the release of negative energy, feelings, and emotions from this energy centre. Breathe in the blue light, and gently breathe out.

Become aware that the waterfall is changing into a soft indigo light and that this light flows directly into your third eye chakra. Let this light vibration gently clear your third eye as the energy flows through every cell of your body, down to your feet. As your third eye chakra fills to overflowing, it allows for the release of negative thoughts, perceptions, and energy that are stored here. Relax as your third eye is cleared and balanced.

We move onto the crown chakra now, as a beautiful lavender light flows down over you and through you. The lavender light fills your crown with a soft and delicate vibration that now envelops you all the way down to your feet.

Stand in this lavender light and ask that the waterfall to wash away all energetic cords from other people as well as any residual energy that has been released from your energy field and chakra system.

Now, step away from the waterfall and join your spirit guide, who is standing by, waiting for you. You can take a few moments to communicate with your guide, asking him or her for clarity and understanding in regards to anything you are unsure of.

When you are ready, thank your spirit guide and walk back along the path to the column of light. Here you will gently float back into your body, realigning your spiritual self with your physical self.

Offer up your green energy mat to be converted into healing energy for Mother Earth.

And now, take a moment to journal your thoughts and feelings. Take note of how you felt during this cleansing and balancing process.

On completion, ask your spirit guide to close down your energy field.

14

Once you choose hope, everything is possible.

CHRISTOPHER REEVES
(1952–2004, AMERICAN ACTOR)

Embracing the Child

As adults, most of us love to be held and comforted by a loved one, friend, or family member. If we feel uncomfortable in this energy, then we must look within to find the reason. Human nature is such that we feel a need to share our lives with others. Yet at times we find ourselves lonely, sad, and despairing, looking for companionship and love but never finding it.

The child within holds the key to whether we allow ourselves to be truly happy or we expect to live a mediocre life, settling for less than we deserve but always yearning for something better. How much we allow is based on the level of self-worth we hold within us. Expectations also play an enormous role in the way our lives play out. What we expect for ourselves is often formed in early childhood, and this energy is stored in our sacral chakra, where self-worth sits.

When we open to healing and allow the light to flow into our physical bodies through the chakra system, we open the door to healing the inner child.

Intentions and Expectations

Much has been written over the years about the power of intention. It is an energy that can be harnessed and projected forward, consciously or unconsciously. It is an energy of planned action, an energy of goal setting and forward thinking. If you intend to do something, whether it is putting out the garbage or washing the dishes, you hold in this intention an expectancy that it will be done. But there is no actual guarantee that the garbage will make it to the front driveway for collection the next morning. If the garbage is to be collected, the intention must become a reality.

It can be heard in many conversations: "I had great intentions this week! I was going to start a new exercise routine; I was going to get up half an hour earlier to meditate; I was going to finally bring balance and order to my life." The next part of the conversation goes like this: "But day one, I had to work late, and the next morning I was too tired, so I slept in. That was the end of my good intentions and rebalancing my life. I will try again next week. Hopefully things will be less busy."

People commence entire years with good intentions; they call them New Year's resolutions! How many New Year's resolutions don't make it to the end of the first week? If a young man or woman decides to give up smoking for good, he or she will harness the good intention by thinking about it, talking about it, and even possibly employing a self-help tool to do it. If the person is told that giving up smoking is easy and that by the end of the month he or she will be nicotine free, there will be the energy of expectation. This is the manifestation of a positive outcome by using forward thinking, planning, and positive expectations.

Unfortunately, we know that in the majority of cases giving up cigarettes is hard. This knowledge then impacts our overall expectations, and failure to quit becomes a reality.

The power to live your life the way you want to live it rests entirely in you. In real terms, you plan your day, your month, and your year. In energetic terms, you can engage positive energy and even call on spiritual assistance to fuel your plans and support you. Herein sits the power of your intentions. The power of your goal setting lies completely in your hands—except the energy of intention can be unsecured and flimsy if not backed by determination, confidence, and hope.

This is where the energy of expectation is different from the energy of intention. If intention is underpinned with expectation, it moves intention higher in terms of vibration but also higher in terms of real effect. When a mother duck waddles off, she expects her ducklings to be behind her, close by and safe. She does not need to harness intention. She has harnessed expectation, and there in her world, what she expects to happen will happen. This is how the power of expectation manifests our reality. Expectation is a powerful thought process that harnesses intention and aligns it with prior knowledge and experience. Intention is the vibration of thinking, planning, and hoping; expectation is the energy of actualising this.

Our mother duck works on the energetic level of expectation and harnesses duck language, movement, and animal instincts to bring her expectations on line. At no time does she doubt her process; she doesn't second-guess her movements. She simply expects that her little brood will follow her, day after day, until the day comes when they have little broods of their own.

If you apply this committed energy to your intention, it shifts you into positive expectation, which in turn allows you to manifest what it is you *think* you want and need. When you expect something to happen, it usually does. When you go to work, you expect much of your day to be sorted, organised, and reliable. You expect the weather channel to be right in its predictions, so you choose your outfit accordingly; you action the weather forecast in your choice of clothing.

You expect the train or the bus to be running on schedule, so you leave the house with plenty of time. You expect the trip will be as boring as usual, so you make sure you don't forget your personal music device! Expectations draw on past experiences and prior knowledge.

If you expect your day to be miserable, then usually it is. This negative expectation will be actualised because of your knowledge of past experiences that are similar and repetitive. Good days and bad days contribute to what you know about life and what you should expect. Listening to other people's opinions and experiences will also contribute to your own expectations.

Family and cultural mores have an enormous impact on what you expect and what you manifest in real terms. Learnt behaviour as a child will endorse many of the proceedings of your life. If you were raised in a violent home with a brutal parent, you will hold expectations that this is typical behaviour for a husband and/or wife. In this energy of expectation, you can very easily attract a violent partner and perpetuate a life of violence and victimisation. If, on the other hand, you were raised in a home with loving and supportive nonviolent parents, you will carry this expectation forward and hopefully attract a similar relationship for yourself.

The power of negative energy is very contagious, because of the nature of our world. People generally fall into the categories of "That would be right! Everything always works out harder for me!" rather than "My day has been as wonderful and fulfilling, as usual!" We have been attuned to negative energy over time, which has desensitised us, and the negative experiences are what we have come to expect. That is why people can be so disbelieving and suspicious when someone does them a good turn.

If only positive energy was as contagious as negative energy!

The concept of paying a good turn forward, or passing on your good fortune, is catching on in some communities. This pay-it-forward energy harnesses good intentions with the expectation of a positive outcome for the receiver, based on personal, positive experiences of the giver.

It becomes apparent, when understanding the power underlying intention and expectation, that you can be programmed for positive outcomes from a very early age. I believe some people default to the positive while others automatically default to the negative. Which side do you vacillate towards? Is your glass always half full or always half empty? Are you an optimist? A pessimist? Or a realist, taking the good with the bad?

The way your life is working or not working for you will be underpinned by your thoughts, perceptions, intentions, and *expectations*. We spoke earlier of the chakra system and the fact that it is your home filing system. Within each chakra you hold onto strong belief patterns and experiences that ultimately drive you forward in every moment of every day. Your life is based on expectations and past experiences that define how you live.

When you bring these aspects of your inner self forward in meditation, you enable healing and spiritual growth from within. Your spirit guide has been in your life from the day you were born and holds witness to all that you have lived through and experienced. Your guide will lead you forward and support your journey with grace, honour, and love.

It is time to open to the world of your inner child. This can be done safely, with loving support, in meditation. The intentions behind your meditation can follow an open-plan experience, or you can go in specifically with a question or problem. This third meditation will take you back to your sacred space, where you will visit with your inner child in the company of your spirit guide.

As you venture within and open a dialogue with your inner child, you will be challenging your long-established *ego-self.* Your ego is the part of you that has managed your life independently up until now. Engaging with your spirit guide and aligning with your higher self, your ego-self will now need to step back to fully allow spiritual growth. This aspect of you is powerful. It has been in charge for years, so you may encounter some roadblocks. My suggestion is to go forward and embrace this wonderful aspect of self with love and understanding.

As you can imagine, there will be many aspects to your inner child. Whatever is bothering you will be brought forward, with the help of your spirit guide. Trust in the process, and open your heart to yourself.

The celestial home meditation gives you the opportunity to develop an effective communication with your inner child. This bridge of love may take some time to build, but with commitment and faith in your own abilities, it will happen.

Your spirit guide knows what it is you are looking for, what it is you want to fix. Patience will be your friend as you open your heart to the child within. Intention will be overlaid with great expectations, and within this safe and supported space, your journey of personal healing and spiritual growth will begin.

The most important thing that you can do is be there in an energy of loving acceptance and nonjudgement for your inner child. If the child is sad, ask why. If the child is angry, ask why. If the child is scared, ask why. If the child is happy, ask why.

You will be accessing your inner child at various stages of development and maturity. You can go to an age that you remember was difficult or traumatic. The power to heal is in your hands, and the power to release the pain and hurt is now up to you.

When your inner children are feeling supported and loved, this energy transfers to you and allows you the benefits of feeling calm and settled, happy, and peaceful.

During this meditation, you will have the opportunity to visit with your *base child*, aged between birth and seven years. During this visit, the inner child can communicate with you by using words, mental images, or memories. The child that comes forward here can be anywhere within that age range. As this line of communication gets stronger and stronger, healing can be accessed. You offer the child understanding, love, and support. The child shows you what it is he or she needs. As the adult in this relationship, you are in charge. You are there to help.

The next child that will come forward is the *sacral child*, aged between seven years and fourteen years. Emotions will run high with this little one. By offering love, understanding, and support, the process of communication and healing will move the adult-you forward to emotional stability and feelings of strong self-worth and assuredness. Be conscious of the images and memories, the emotions and the feelings, as you open this aspect of yourself up for healing.

Also during this meditation, you will access the *solar plexus child*, aged fourteen to twenty-one years. This aspect of you sits in the solar plexus and is aligned with your feelings of self-esteem, self-determination, and self-control. As you learn more about yourself and remember the challenges you faced during those years, you will grow into a stronger, more self-confident person.

The Celestial Home meditation allows the adult-you to build strong, loving foundations with the inner children. Be courageous and brave with this process as you open up memories of challenging times or relationships. It is the conscious awareness of these setbacks that allows them to rise to the surface for healing and acceptance. Keeping things buried and hidden works against us you every level, creating illness, depression, and even disease. Meditation and healing will take you on a path of health and happiness.

Remember that your spirit guide is facilitating this meditation and communication. Trust that what you see is real. Even if it does not make sense at first, stay focused and go with it. It is very easy to second-guess the meditation. The ego-self loves to interfere, especially when change and healing are afoot. The ego-self prefers to keep things the same. Your biggest challenges will come from within, so stay determined and strive forward to healing and success.

CELESTIAL HOME

The Celestial Home Meditation

Begin your meditation with your prayers of protection (page 87).

As you sit in a comfortable upright position, bring down a column of brilliant white light.

Breathe this light in through your nose and out through your mouth, relaxing more and more with each breath.

See and feel this white-light energy flow over you and through you, all the way down to your feet. Breathe it in as it gently flows into every cell of your body.

Continue with your breathing as you become aware of a soft but vibrant green light moving into the column of energy. See the green light form an energy mat at your feet. As you relax into this energy, feel yourself gently floating upwards into the green light. Float slowly up towards your sacred space.

As you stand on the vibrant green grass, look around at this magnificent space that you have created for yourself out of love and light. Enjoy the feelings of peace, harmony, and security as you look around at the trees, the gardens, and the meadows. Everything here is beautiful, just as you expect it to be.

Your spirit guide joins you here, taking your hand and guiding you forward.

As you look around, you notice a lovely house over in the distance. You are guided along a path towards this home. It is your heavenly home, and it is designed exactly how you want it to be.

Your spirit guide takes you up to the front door. You are going to visit three bedrooms today and meet three different parts of yourself.

The first room is the red room; it is decorated is shades of red and pink. In this room you are greeted by a small child waiting to speak to you. This young aspect of you is aged between one and seven years old. This child is aligned with your base chakra.

Step into the room with your spirit guide and greet the child. Sit with this child, talk to him or her, and offer your help. Ask the child how he/she is feeling and whether there is anything needed or wanted.

This small child may give you something or may want something. Whatever it is, be grateful and loving in this exchange.

Now it is time to walk to the next room and visit with the child in the orange bedroom. Take time to talk with this child, asking questions and offering love and support. The child in this room is aged between seven years and fourteen years and is aligned with the sacral chakra. Again, you may be given a gift or an awareness; be loving and grateful in this exchange.

The next room is the yellow bedroom. This child greets you and gives you the opportunity to support him or her and offer healing. Take time to sit and get to know this aspect of you. The child here is aged between fourteen years and twenty-one. These are the teenage years during which we grow into young adulthood. This aspect of you is aligned with the solar plexus chakra.

When you are ready, invite all the three aspects of you (the inner children) into the living room of your beautiful celestial home. Your spirit guide has planned a lovely celebration for you all. Enjoy this time as the inner children are showered with love and light from this being of light.

It is time to say goodbye to the inner children now, so take a moment to embrace each one, offering them words of loving acceptance, nonjudgement, and support. Let them know that you will be back to visit them all soon.

In the company of your spirit guide, walk back along the grassy green path until you arrive back to the column of green light. Step into his column and gently flow back into your body, realigning your spiritual self with your physical self.

Take time to journal this profound experience. Try to remember each of the exchanges with the inner children. Also, take note of how you felt during this meditation.

On completion, offer up your green energy mat to be converted into healing energy for Mother Earth. Then ask your spirit guide to close down your energy field.

Through the healing process in meditation, you engage your higher self and spirit guide for healing and awareness. When the chakra system is clearing, you undergo a number of releases from this life experience as well as from past lives. By working with your inner child in the celestial home meditation, you become able to manage difficult situations that would normally cause anxiety, fear, anger, and frustration.

To maintain a strong, powerful, and pure connection to your higher self, you need to stay out of ego and lower self. Sometimes this is difficult because of the nature of the healing process, especially when deeply held negative emotions are being released.

The solar plexus is the seat of your soul; it is where your power sits. If this power is aligned with your higher self through your spirit guide, then you feel calm, confident, and self-assured. Your life flows easily. You have no trouble making decisions, and you feel strong in your convictions.

When life throws you a challenge, you can either give it to your higher self—"holding your form"—or you can try to control it, like grabbing a raging bull by the horns. When this doesn't work, mistrust, fear, and old limiting belief patterns slip in, and you lose sight of your higher self and guidance. Then you slide down into the fifteen-year-old self who wants to control your life anyway. And you keep everything the same.

Now the arrogant teenager who thinks she/he knows everything takes over. Once the fifteen-year-old realises one cannot hold a raging bull, she/he panics. This is when you slide into the emotional body and into the sea of doubt and confusion. From here you take up residence in the base chakra and run your world from the perspective of the lonely six-year-old, who has become a victim of circumstances, with no power to change.

At this point, your higher self and spirit guide are waving to you from a long way away, unable to convince you that you don't have to do this alone. The bull has become your companion, as the two of you sit on the grass feeling alone but relatively safe.

The bull represents life's challenges and obstacles: grief, loss, financial struggles, mean and hurtful people, failed relationships, sickness, ill health, and so on. It is okay to make friends with the bull; in fact, you need to stare the bull down right between the eyes. But do it from your higher-self energy of love, compassion, forgiveness, and trust. When you sit in self-love, self-acceptance, and joy, the bull becomes your friend and a gift to learn from.

The *negative ego* is the part of you that thinks you are better than others—stronger, more spiritual, in charge. When you use your power to control the outcome and manipulate people, ask yourself, "Why does my fifteen-year-old self need to be in control of this situation?" By handing the situation over to your spirit guide and higher self, you will open your energy to light and love. This energy will calm the ego and offer feelings of peace and harmony, allowing you to relax and let go.

Your higher self sees you as unique, courageous, and special, but this awareness comes from you, to you. It does not need to be validated by comparing yourself to others. When you are in emotional turmoil—fear, anxiety, or confusion—your eight-year-old self is in charge, the part of you that is connected to the world through your emotional body.

As we heal our past and current lives, we need to keep our emotions balanced and calm. Fear and panic need to be addressed. Anger needs to be addressed; sadness needs to be addressed. If these emotions remain unchecked, then the slide to lower self takes place. And the six-year-old controls everything from a safe and secure hole in the ground!

SPIRITUAL HOUSEWORK

123

15

The best and safest thing is to keep a balance in your life, acknowledge the great powers around us and in us. If you can do that, and live that way, you are really a wise man.

EURIPIDES
(480 TO 406 BC, ANCIENT GREEK PHILOSOPHER)

Spiritual Housework: Helping Ourselves and Mother Earth

Cleansing and balancing the energy within your home helps to create a peaceful refuge from the chaos of the world outside. Through the process of meditation, you build the light energy within your physical body. You bring balance and clarity to your emotions and open up the pathway of light to a bright and wonderful future.

As you clear and heal your own energy field through meditation, you will become more sensitive to negative energy. You will feel when something is not right. Traditional space-clearing methods, such as music, candles, and smudging, can assist in creating a nice ambience in your home as well as raise the vibration of the space. But by working with light energy through your spirit guide and the angelic realm, you will find the results much more effective.

Simply follow these guidelines, and your home will be an energetic asset to you and your loved ones. It is always preferable to cleanse and balance your home when you are home on your own.

Begin by saying your prayer and aligning yourself with your spirit guide.

Ask your spirit guide to dress you in the appropriate armour of protection that you need, from the top of your head down to your feet. Stand in the centre of your home, and bring down a column of brilliant white light.

State your intention. "I wish to cleanse and clear my home, bringing the energy of this house into balance and alignment with me and in harmony with Mother Earth."

Ask that all pets, crystals, jewellery, and plants be encased in bubbles of gold.

Now ask your spirit guide to bring forward the appropriate angelic assistance to align with your house, to raise its vibration and also to provide your home with protection.

Begin by asking your spirit guide to place a wall of **golden bricks** around the perimeter of your home and on internal walls, ceilings, and floors. See these golden bricks with your mind's eye; imagine them throughout the home, covering floors, ceilings, and walls.

See now a vibrant green energy mat flowing over all the floor surfaces like a lush green carpet.

With your spirit guide's assistance, ask your house angel to shut down all the doors between dimensions and repair any dimensional tears that have been created in your home over time. These tears can occur in heavy traffic areas as well as busy rooms. The repair of these tears will allow the energy in your home to build without leaking away.

It is quite common for lost souls to take up residence in homes. These souls move through the lower astrals, often entering homes and buildings through portholes or tears in the dimensional walls. They drain the energy in the home and, on the rare occasion, create mischief to unsettle the occupants. The removal of these souls must be done with the help of the angelic presence. Lost souls need to be returned to their place of origin. By smudging and burning candles you might move souls to another house or room, but they will not cross over into the light without angelic assistance.

So, you will work with your spirit guide to assist with the removal of any souls that are lost or dwelling in your home. Ask for the angelic assistance to come down in a column of white light. Tell them, "You do not belong in this dimension, and you do not have permission to stay in my home. Go now, and return into the light, to the original source of your soul. Go with love!" The lost souls will be gathered by the angels and gently crossed over. They will travel up into the column of light provided for them. The lost souls will be escorted to the healing level appropriate for them in the upper astral plane.

If you feel resistance, ask for a golden net to collect any entities or souls that are refusing to cross. If a soul refuses to leave, state the following: "If you continue to stay in my home, you do so without my permission. You will be accountable for your actions in the hall of justice, under the jurisdiction of Archangel Michael." This statement is very powerful, and most souls will acknowledge this truth and go into the light.

When you feel satisfied that all unwanted visitors have been crossed into the light, take the next step. Ask your spirit guide to provide a **column of cleansing light** that will gently move through every room in your home, removing negative and dense energy. Walk methodically from room to room, visualising the column gently spinning and vacuuming all of the negative energy. The column will move through furniture, beds, lounges, and all solid objects and linens. Pay particular attention to the beds, TVs, computers, computer games, etc.

When this is done, bring yourself back to your central location and ask for this column of light to be sent back up, with angelic help, and converted into positive healing energy for Planet Earth. If any room feels as if it needs more attention, go back and work with the column of light again. Be patient, and you will feel the shift of energy.

Place **blue energy curtains** over each window and all the doors. Finally, ask the angelic assistance to create a curtain-like structure, a **wall of gold and white light** around your entire property. This curtain of white and gold light will protect your home and assist with the building of the light energy within the property.

If you live in an apartment or a home that is attached to another building, work with your spirit guide and the angelic assistance to build the protective curtain between the common walls, ceilings, and floors of your home. Thereby you will be separating your home from others.

Stand now with your spirit guide, and top yourself up with white light from the top of your head down to your feet. State firmly, "I claim this home in my name and in the name of Divine Creator for the light!" See and feel the light expanding throughout your entire home.

On completion of your house clearing, thank your spirit guide and all who have assisted. You can now ask that the columns of cleansing energy be sent back up and converted into positive healing energy for Mother Earth. Ask your spirit guide to bring down golden spinning hoops of protection for you now.

It would be appropriate as well to light a candle or burn a favourite aromatherapy oil. To expand the building of love and light in your home, continue to do house clearings on a regular basis. You and your loved ones will truly benefit from this work.

Your spirit guide will orchestrate the house clearing and will engage the appropriate help from the angelic realm to support your requests and needs. It is always relevant to clear the energy of arguments, sadness, grief, or even visitors. Doing regular clearings at home will allow you to truly own the space, and your private oasis will support you with energy of peace, comfort, and harmony.

By cleansing and balancing our physical worlds, we are assisting Mother Earth in so many ways. The negative energy that she needs to process is enormous, and our efforts in transmuting negative energy to positive energy allow us to lighten her load. Our Garden of Eden is under pressure from population growth, industry, mining, overfishing, and deforestation. Let us all try a little to change our physical world for the better, thereby creating a ripple effect of light waves that float in every direction, across our lands and oceans.

16

I learned that courage was not the absence
of fear, but the triumph over it.

NELSON MANDELA
(1918–2013, SOUTH AFRICAN PRESIDENT,
ACTIVIST, AND PHILANTHROPIST)

Fertile Ground

As we stay with our Garden of Eden theme, I wish to open us to the conversation around personal trauma and stored negative energy in detail. In the first few pages of this book I discussed that earth is our Garden of Eden, where souls come to grow. Due to circumstances and life choices, souls sometimes live in undernourished soil, with no light or hope, and so the souls simply manage to survive for a time. Other souls find themselves planted in sunny, open fields of light, warmth, and fertile soil. Under these circumstances these souls blossom and grow.

Another aspect to life is the interference and influence of others on our somewhat perfect existence. People suffer abuse, violence, accidents, addictions, and disease. These negative elements can change the path and soul purpose for an individual, creating a life of dysfunction and hopelessness.

When a soul is born into poverty and disharmony, we must assume these choices were made by the soul in conjunction with the guidance of the councils, in order to fulfil a life lesson or spiritual growth through adversity. A soul who has lived previous lives of wealth, health, and happiness may consciously choose to experience starvation and poverty to know what this is like and to raise its vibration through learning and acceptance. In this way the soul will embrace empathy and compassion for humanity.

When a soul is on an evolutionary path, it is necessary to empathise and understand the challenges of being human. This makes us better people in the long term. We must move through adversity and hardship with grace, gratitude, and humility.

Now, on the other hand, we have souls on earth with well-thought-out plans, orchestrated to bring light onto Planet Earth by their lives of goodness. These lives can be complex as well as simple. The complex version will entail leadership qualities, intelligent and inquiring minds, integrity, compassion, innovation, enthusiasm, gifts and talents, as well as a true devotion to the highest good of all life on earth.

A simple life lived in the light will impact at a ground level. It will move through communities and villages, towns, and cities as a profound energy of goodness, kindness, compassion, integrity, honesty, generosity, and love. There are many levels of existence within the complex and simple aspects of our world. If given the green light, earth would be a wonderful place for everyone. The energies of goodness would filter through to every living thing.

However, the reality of our world is impacted by negativity every day. Over the centuries war has raged, and we still carry within our emotional bodies aspects of battles we have lived through in past lives. Earth itself holds these violent memories, places where battles have been fought on her soil. Yet earth is identified as an emotional planet, where healing of the soul becomes possible. If we heal the negative emotions associated with past-life trauma and present-life trauma, we can open the pathway back to the light. In the process, we can heal the planet.

If a person is blessed with a loving family and positive, nurturing, and sustaining energy, the fertile soil within his energy field is strong and supports the growth of love and light. This will continue in positive ways, but it can be interrupted if a trauma happens or an accident. Then the fertile ground is darkened and the light is dimmed, creating another type of fertile soil, where negative thoughts and fear grow.

Fear is an essential ingredient for negative-fertile ground. Negative thoughts become weeds in the sacral chakra and block the person from moving on to challenging and exciting experiences. The negative self-talk comes from deep within, and the darkness grows. These thoughts can be influenced by others: parents, siblings, or even friends. Once the person believes this dialogue, the negative self feeds the fertile ground and the weeds block the flow of light. What you believe, you become.

Societies, governments, and the media have a very big part to play in the perpetuation of fear. The need to control most of the world's population is apparent, and the world governments stay in control when fear is present. The media loves to fill us with fear—what used to be a normal winter's day with a cold snap now becomes described as an "Arctic vortex"! Even reporting on the weather has become a fear-based industry.

Incidents that have occurred in childhood can be stored as negative energy and memories. This energy is ignited when a similar experience comes along later in life. The adult self reverts back to the emotions and trauma of the child in order to deal with the situation. The adult behaves in an emotionally immature manner, acting out as a child would. When two adults are responding from inner-child emotion, the situation resembles schoolyard behaviours—it can even resemble three-year-olds fighting in the sandpit over a bucket and spade!

A client recently described to me the way she collapses emotionally if people raise their voices to her or disapprove of her verbally. She becomes extremely upset and withdraws from the situation at hand, without any resolution for either person. In her healing session, we identified her eleven-year-old child as being the most vulnerable in these situations. She remembers a pivotal time when her mother berated her loudly and aggressively for something she had done wrong. This energetic attack impacted heavily on her self-worth at the time, and it was making it extremely difficult for her to be assertive, mature, and self-assured when confronted by verbal aggression in her workplace now.

In her healing session, we brought this memory and similar experiences up for conversation. We worked on healing the young eleven-year-old girl who was feeding this negative-fertile ground. When we align with the spirit guides, we are aligning with witnesses to the trauma. With the spirit guides' help, it is sometimes simply a matter of acknowledging the emotional trauma in order to release it with love and light.

In another session, a young wife came to discuss her marriage. Her husband was demonstrating "bully" energy towards her and her young children. His behaviour was getting more and more aggressive, and she was genuinely concerned for the future of her marriage. His father had died suddenly when her husband was twelve years old. He was the oldest of five children. His mother had been traumatised and devastated by the death of her husband and had placed all her hopes and expectations on her oldest son. She'd told him he was the man of the house now.

This young boy had taken on this role by becoming aggressive and controlling towards his siblings. He pushed them around and ordered them to do odd jobs and pull their weight in the household. His mother gave him free reign as she withdrew from family responsibility and guidance. This boy was suffering his own loss of his dad, and these sad and negative emotions fuelled his anger and despair. This negativity was projected towards his younger brothers and sisters.

His life continued in the same way until he married and had children of his own. The only way he knew to control anything was through using the aggressive, bullying behaviour that he'd learnt when he was twelve years old. The way forward for this young father would be to follow a path of grief counselling and healing. His fertile ground was choking the love and light in his life with masses of weeds, full of sadness and loss. He needed to be shown love and compassion; he also needed an enormous amount of acceptance and understanding.

With this understanding, my client went home to begin to rebuild her marriage. She had a new awareness and level of compassion for the emotional trauma her husband had experienced as a small boy, and she realised that love and compassion were what he needed most.

To ensure your fertile ground is seeded with love and light, it is essential that you go within and find your truth. Gently open your memory bank with regard to traumas, accidents, and illnesses. Talk to your spirit guide about these memories in your meditations and ask for healing. It is very possible to clear your negative-fertile ground and replace it with a wonderful garden of light love.

Adversaries can also interfere with our well-made plans, and sometimes these souls follow us from life to life. Soul contracts are usually involved in relationships, but it is never okay to cause someone pain or anguish. Adversaries can be very close; they can be disguised as very best friends, business colleagues, or family members. It does not always make sense. Our rational minds are very good at overriding our intuition, but when we observe patterns of behaviour, then it is possible to shine the light on an old enemy and deal with the truth.

A good example is when a friend always pips you at the post—going for the same job as you, going out with your ex, taking over your life, or following your every move in order to get in first. You may think this is just the way it is and no big deal. However, when you look a little closer, certain signs start to appear. The cracks open up in your friendship when you challenge the status quo. People who are insecure often ride on the coat-tails of others. It is not always concerning, but people such as these can drag you off path and slow down your journey to happiness and well-being.

> *It takes a great deal of bravery to stand up to our enemies*
> *but just as much to stand up to our friends.*
> ——
> JK ROWLING (UK AUTHOR)

I like to encourage people to take of their "rose-coloured" glasses and look beyond the façade, to see the truth. Jealously, envy, and covetousness are some of the nastier energies that are projected between friends and family. Maligning gossip and ill-wishing are just as bad. I recommend that you observe the behaviours of people— how they act and what they say and, of course how, they say it and to whom.

Become discerning about whom you spend time with. Gather people around you who love and care about you, who support you and offer words of wisdom and guidance. Surrounding yourself with trustworthy and honest people is the way forward into the light. Your circle of friends and acquaintances may shrink a little, but it's the quality of the friends that is important, not the quantity.

Speaking of "friends" ... social media is a challenging forum. Depending on how you use it, it is possible to open your world up for everyone to see. Personally and professionally, people are exposing themselves to an enormous energy that is very difficult to filter and control. Be aware of your personal space and who you wish to share it with. Build a wall of light around yourself, and be clever about your positioning in the world.

I feel social media is a way of receiving external validation from your peers in an artificial manner. When you truly love and accept yourself, you only need validation from within. The social media form of personal exposure is not healthy, and I wonder what the long-term ramifications will be, socially and personally. There exists an ethical dilemma within these forums. It is up to you as an individual to monitor your own behaviours. The element of voyeurism and the distance created by the unseen matrix of the internet allows some individuals to do and say things they would not normally do or say.

Never before has society been so privy to what is happening in everyone's lives. What happened to the old slide night when you came back from holidays? All your friends and family would get together to welcome you home, share a meal, and look at your holiday pics! In today's Facebook and Instagram world, people are virtually on holiday with you. Privacy is something to be valued and treasured. It allows you to build a world of light and love without being challenged.

My suggestion is to keep contact with immediate friends and family and refrain from attempting to build "Facebook friends" so you feel good about yourself. Love from your spirit guide and love of self brings with it untold waves of good feelings! Be clever about your choices, especially when putting yourself out into the World Wide Web.

Part 3

Light Working!

17

Choosing Goodness

If you were to write a list of your top-ten *good* people, where would you start? Firstly, how would you define *goodness*?

What makes a person good?

Let's agree that in regards to people, *good* means decent, respectable, moral, virtuous, honest, generous, reliable, helpful, trustworthy, courteous, kind, and considerate. Someone you know may hold some of these traits or maybe all!

I believe you can see it in their eyes. Goodness shines through. You can feel it in their presence; goodness makes *you* feel better. You witness it in the actions of good people, by what they do and how they do it. Goodness is something to aspire to. In our world, being a good person is all that really matters.

My journey as a healer and writer is about bringing out the goodness in a person, shining the light on the inside to clear the way for goodness to take hold.

I believe the journey back to the Creator must take the path of goodness. We are not isolated from each other, we are part of an energetic matrix that links us all. As one soul clears the path to a life filled with light and love, goodness can spread and, as with the pebble in the stream, move outwards in concentric circles of hope for humanity.

As love is an energy with an eternal source, so is goodness. At its highest vibration, goodness can make a difference to all of us. I suppose we can reflect on the meaning of *badness* and realize the detrimental effects bad people and actions have on communities and families. However, we cannot dwell on the negativity if we wish to fill our lives with light and love.

As I am writing this chapter, an area west of Sydney is suffering the ravages of bush fires. Around two hundred homes have been destroyed, people's lives have been shattered, and hope for many has been lost. Within this nightmare, goodness has shone through. The genuine and courageous efforts made by the Fire Service volunteers and their professional fire-fighting colleagues has been awe inspiring.

The generosity from person to person has been incredibly heart-warming, and yet in the midst of all this wonderful goodness, there is a small element of evil—looters and thieves! It is beyond belief for most people that someone could enter a home or shop and steal while others are suffering. It is also unbelievable that arsonists will deliberately light fires and then join the fire crews to help put them out.

At times like these, we must focus on the good people and their generosity; we must not give oxygen to the bad deeds of the minority.

Children represent goodness at the highest vibration. Sometimes they can be mischievous or disobedient, but within their authentic nature, goodness shines through.

It is worthwhile to take a moment and write your list of ten good people you know. In your journal, write down the attributes that you admire the most in these people. Attributes such as honesty, selflessness, kindness, and thoughtfulness are high on my list. And there are the people who are simply good through and through.

My mother-in-law Daphne was one such lady. She delighted in greeting you every time you saw her. She cared about people and cared for people. She always had a smile and was the first person to lend a hand. Daphne was a country girl, raised with wonderful values from hard-working parents. She is dearly missed by her children and grandchildren.

Take a moment now to focus on yourself. What are the attributes within yourself that you recognise as good? For now, stay away from your physical blessings! We are talking about the soul self, the personality traits and the genuine aspects of self that can be shared with others in unlimited supply. Goodness comes from the heart; it is spontaneous and true.

In prayers and meditation, we can call on Spirit to bring something to fruition for the *highest good*. This request allows for the blessings of Spirit to fall onto the shoulders of those most worthy. Expectations and deservedness play an important role here. If someone is due for a blessing, then she can receive it if her heart is open and she feels deserving of the gift.

For example, if a young girl has processed healing around her feelings of self-worth and has been working hard in her job for a promotion, then she will be able to receive the blessings of good fortune. On the other hand, if she is hanging onto old negative energies associated with previous job experiences and low self-worth, she will be quite capable of blocking the good as if flows towards her. The job she was hoping for could be offered to someone else. Her negative-fertile ground will have a major impact.

As we offer light and love for the highest good to others, we must also understand that it will be received by those who are energetically on track to receive. People who exist in a state of negativity, fear, and upset won't recognise the energy, and through the laws of attraction, it will move onto someone who does. Thus the healing process of clearing blockages and negativity is paramount to accessing all the blessings that living on earth can offer. The higher self of each individual connects to the source of love and light and also resonates at *goodness*. When a person is aligned with his higher self, his life flows easily, and *goodness* is an important and essential part of his day. Goodness flows through him; it shines through the eyes of the higher self and into the soul energy of the individual. The higher self is nonjudgemental, loving, kind, and thoughtful. The more of this energy that flows through into a person's life the more good is allowed in.

Your spirit guide is your conduit to your higher self. The spirit guide is a being of light and love who filters your higher self-energy in adjustable amounts so you can assimilate this energy and raise your vibration. The more contact and communication you have with your spirit guide the stronger your connection to your higher self will become. Your higher self is your direct connection to the energy of the Divine Creator while you live here on earth. Your spirit guide, in the correct order of light, opens and supports this loving connection.

By communicating with your spirit guide each day, you will open the flow of this wonderful loving energy. In this heightened space, you will be inclined to make better choices that support your highest good and the highest good of others. When you are not sure about something, go within, and trust your feelings. If a decision feels good and right, then you know you are on your path.

Alternatively, if something feels bad or wrong, stop. Call in your spirit guide to support you in the moment and help you decide. From an accountability perspective, it will always be important to act in the interest of goodness, kindness, and love. However, the choice will always be up to you. Remember that on this earth plane free will and choice is our right. Your spirit guide cannot and will not override any decision you make.

So, choose goodness, choose kindness, and choose the right path for the highest good of all. When the energy of *good* is aligned with and shared with many souls, anything is possible.

18

Good actions give strength to ourselves and
inspire good actions in others.

———

PLATO
(428BC–348BC, ANCIENT GREEK PHILOSOPHER)

Growing Your Soul Self

One of the biggest challenges to spiritual growth is the release of the ego self to the higher self. Our personality parts identify us as the persons in body at this time and space. And of course, this is true. My meet-and-greet personality part is represented as Jennifer. People know me as Jennifer and think of me as Jennifer. However, Jennifer is a current amalgamation of my past life experiences, my authentic self, and my ego self, as well as my higher self.

It is my connection to my authentic self that has allowed the flow of my higher self into this life, and in this flow, my ego-self steps back. It doesn't make me less powerful as Jennifer. In fact, it makes me more powerful, because I allow my higher self in to assist with my life path. I have chosen to let go of the strings and let my higher self take charge.

The ability to do this requires practice, faith, and patience—especially because things don't always happen when we want them to or expect them to. At other times, when things seem to happen miraculously, it is because we have let go of the controls and forgotten about the issue. Forgetting about the request or situation will allow our higher selves and spirit guides the opportunity to work in the higher realms without hindrance.

If we keep asking and praying for the same thing repeatedly, we affirm that we do not trust that our request has been heard. Then our ego-selves step back in to take charge. Our spirit guides and higher selves get pushed back by the determined ego-selves. Once a request has been petitioned in meditation or prayer, we must give it time to come into fruition—without constant interference from the lower, untrusting self.

However, we must be understanding of the ego-lower self, because this part of our psychology and energetic make-up has been in charge all these years and has gotten us to this current time and space. The lower self can be stubborn and difficult to budge.

This is where meditations will help. The inner child represents the energy of the lower self. It is very powerful in controlling outcomes, particularly if past events have played a big part in shaping your emotional body. The lower self holds onto fear, anxiety, trepidation, lack of confidence, low self-worth, and doubt. In order to give up your power to your spirit guide and higher self, the lower self must be aligned with faith and hope and great expectations of joy. This is when you can engage with a wonderful partnership of higher self-wisdom and spirit guidance, thereby allowing your ego self to be filled with trust and confidence

This alignment is possible through the healing meditations in the celestial home. When you take your conscious mind into this space to visit your inner children, you will build a bridge of strength and light. Your goal is to view your child in the solar plexus as relaxed, calm, and confident. To reach this goal, the base child and the sacral child will both need to be lovingly supported by you.

Understanding and remembering life's challenges allows for the loving energy of forgiveness to flow into your inner child—forgiveness for yourself as well as others.

Spiritual and Lifelong Goals.

As we establish our spiritual and life goals, we can embark on a meditation path that heightens our awareness and brings us understanding and acceptance. However, goals cannot be achieved without a solid plan of action. Our plan of action needs to be built around a daily schedule and the wheel-of-life balance.

The pie chart of life is made up of a few regular sectors. These include health and well-being, recreation, work/career, relationships, spiritual development, self-time, and financial freedom. Each of these sectors relates directly to the chakra system and can be made strong and healthy through regular energy work.

As our chakras are cleansed and balanced, they begin to open and allow the release of negative emotions, feelings, and thoughts that have been stored over time. The release of these negative energies will assist us to become the persons we want to be, living satisfying, healthy, and purposeful lives. In this space, meditation is the key to growth.

Let us revisit the chakra system. Building on what we already know, we begin with the **base chakra** elements. Here we need to provide ourselves with a home and basic supplies. This is essential. We need clothing, warmth, and sustenance for physical survival. We need boundaries to feel safe and secure. We need to fertilise our soil well at this level, so we can grow happy, healthy lives. To activate and strengthen the base chakra, we must cultivate patience and allow things to come around in time. Trust and faith determine the level of patience we have.

Let us create a structure that supports our lifestyle choices and maintains stability and continuity through routines and planning. We must trust in the innate goodness of life on earth and be grateful for small things!

As we know, this chakra is aligned with the energy of Mother and Mother Earth. Some of us were not nurtured and loved as we would have liked to be. Let us find ways to be kind to ourselves and to mother ourselves through self-nurturing routines. We'll make sure our cupboards are always full of the basic necessities, so that when we arrive home we will feel welcomed and provided for.

Next is to create a physical space at home and work that is clean, tidy, and free of clutter. We honour ourselves by maintaining healthy bodies and healthy homes.

Using our meditations to heal and strengthen our relationships with our mothers will also make us feel secure and loved. The Celestial Home meditation will be of immense help. Finding time for ourselves in our busy world will allow us to sustain and nurture a loving relationship with ourselves. This is the basis of our journey on earth, the journey to loving ourselves without conditions.

Affirmations are words of encouragement that foster new, positive belief patterns. They work particularly well when they truly resonate with our personal truths. In time, they will override negative beliefs and set us up for paths of success. Affirmations need to feel right. We will focus on the words and hold them in our hearts.

Here are some positive affirmations for the base chakra:

I am always in the right place at the right time!
Wherever I am, God is, and all is well.
I exist in this divine time and space; I belong here and now.
I love my life and manifest my heart's desires.
I have everything I want and need within me now.
My life reflects my true self; I am goodness and light.

The **sacral chakra** governs *how* we live our lives. It is here that we embrace quality and quantity. Our lives are a representation of what we truly believe we deserve, and this deservedness governs our attitudes to the acceptance of good.

The sacral chakra is ruled by emotion and is best supported by a balanced lifestyle. It is here that we honour the needs of the physical body through the life experiences of pleasure. The amount of pleasure we allow ourselves is directly connected to self-worth. To help balance the wheel of life, we must make time in our daily schedules for pleasure, fun, and recreation.

We focus on making positive lifestyle choices that enhance our well-being and good health. We value our physical bodies by taking care of them. We honour our physical home and workplace by keeping order, housekeeping, and by arranging beautiful, aesthetic environments.

The sacral chakra is the home to career, finance, and the flow of abundance. It is also tied directly to the energy of father and provider. Some people find that money flows easily in and out of their lives, while others have a continuous struggle to stay financially secure. Our belief systems about money sit firmly in the sacral, and these will define the quality of our lives in terms of financial freedom.

To raise our self-worth, we meditate with our inner child and regularly cleanse and balance our chakra systems in meditation. It is always relevant to heal father-child relationships. These meditations will ensure that our emotional bodies strengthen and bring forward more of our hearts' desires.

We treat ourselves to enjoyable pastimes such a long walks, swimming, massage, and movies. As we experience the joys of this life, our levels of self-worth are ignited and reinforced by our divine sense of self.

A strong sacral chakra allows us to view the world from a glass-half-full perspective and not the other way around. As part of a healthy wheel-of-life balance, we must remember to stop and smell the roses.

Here are some positive affirmations for the sacral chakra:

**I exist in the flow of the divine creator; I feel good.
I am worth my weight in gold, and I allow the abundance
of the universe to flow easily and freely into my life.
The abundance of the universe now aligns
with my truth and integrity.
I attract positive experiences and joy through
my positive expectations and hope.
I deserve all that is positive on offer for me today.**

The **solar plexus** essentially governs choices. It is where our intuition sits and guides us to choose one way or the other. It is also the seat of the soul, so the clearer and more balanced the solar plexus, the easier it is to make positive choices in life. This chakra develops between the ages of fourteen years and twenty-one years, a time of life when we are moving into adulthood and thinking about our futures. If during this time you were muddled or off track, it is very possible your solar plexus isn't as strong as it should be. Also, consider that over our lifetimes we have been influenced by the people around us, and this influence co-creates our adult selves.

Limiting belief patterns and self-esteem determine what we truly believe we can achieve in life. Our personal power, or lack of it, sits in the solar plexus. This is the ego self, the seat of our individual personalities. When the solar plexus is in balance, the ego is strong and effective and confirmed in worthiness and confidence. The need to control and manipulate others does not exist. Balancing the solar plexus comes from knowing and loving your true and authentic self.

Spending time alone helps develop a true sense of self, as does identifying our gifts and talents and making choices that demonstrate positive self-esteem and self-worth. When we rise to the challenge and dig deep into our personal resources, we strengthen and balance the solar plexus. Finding our courageous selves will build our character and self-esteem.

When we simply complete a task, we are affirming our truths. We can pat ourselves on the back! We can smile and feel good.

The solar plexus brings balance to the wheel of life by encouraging positive choices towards study and education as well as time management and organisation. It is a centre of action, planning, goal setting, and inspiration. Learning and education raises our social awareness and gives us a perspective on the world. The more we learn, the more we know!

Here are some positive affirmations to support the solar plexus:

I know who I am; I acknowledge my true and authentic self.
I make inspired and guided choices that are for my highest good.
I trust and believe in myself.
I hold the power of my divine creator in my soul.
I understand and accept myself on all levels of my existence.
I choose goodness and light.

The **heart chakra** is the centre of love and vitality. This chakra is the centre of our lives physically and spiritually, and it is essential to life on many levels. Our hearts are nourished by peace and harmony and are strengthened by love and light.

The ability of the heart to open to unconditional love from others, as well as from the Divine Source, will depend on how the heart is seeded. This seeding happens during the earliest years of life. So, if the infant child is loved and nurtured in secure surroundings, its ability to love the life it is living is very real.

However, if the child is struggling to survive, and the flow of love is scarce and conditional, the ability of this child's heart to openly receive love and give love will be compromised.

Nonetheless, the heart can be grown in our Garden of Eden, if it is fertilised with love and forgiveness.

Loving yourself is key to growing your heart chakra, and the more you love yourself without conditions, the more the people in your life will reflect this love. Begin each day with a smile on your face and a positive affirmation.

As you contribute to the well-being of others, through kindness and compassion, you automatically feel good about yourself. Forgiveness is also the key to loving yourself, forgiveness of self as well as others. Let yourself off the hook occasionally. Be kind to yourself and nonjudgemental of your own actions.

Find the time to do what you love with the people you love. Have fun and have a laugh. Spend time with people who inspire you and support you. Validate yourself, and relax!

When you create a peaceful and nurturing home, you love being there. Take the time to clean, declutter, and decorate your home. Injecting your personal space with love and light will ensure a welcoming and supportive home environment for you to blossom in.

Here are some positive affirmations for the heart chakra:

**I love and accept myself without condition,
on every level of my existence.
I choose to live my life with love and grace.
I am a vessel of love and light.
I choose to share my love and light.
I love my life and the journey I am on.
I allow the love of my divine creator to flow into my heart today.**

The throat chakra is our centre of communication in the physical world as well as in the spiritual world. It is the gateway to the higher consciousness; it needs to be strong, open, and free-flowing. Honesty and truth are the key ingredients to maintaining a healthy throat chakra. Damage to this chakra can be done through negative energy, malicious gossip, and lies. The fabric of the throat charka is fine and delicate and is often the first gateway for illnesses such as colds and flu to attack the physical body.

This chakra is aligned with integrity as well as will power. By developing a strong relationship with your personal truth, you bring about a healthy and strong throat chakra. As one of the souls living here on earth, you are blessed with free will and choice. In order to activate this blessing, you must be tuned into your inner truth and be open to guidance from above. Being self-assured and assertive allows for establishing free will, and when you are open to spiritual guidance, you make decisions that support your highest good. Staying calm and assertive in a tricky situation allows for angry and aggressive confrontations to be diluted and managed.

You begin your own personal road to empowerment when you tell the truth and acknowledge the truth about yourself. The truth is not always good, but the truth is the truth! Learning to love and forgive yourself and others, despite the truth, often brings about confrontation, but at the same time it is very liberating.

You should always strive to be honest and truthful in any given situation and to express emotions with honest words. Writing letters to significant people allows you to release difficult emotions that have been buried deep within. You don't need to send these letters! The healing comes through the process of writing and expressing the truth about how you feel. As this energy is released with love, it flows back to you in time as a gift. The negative energy between you and the significant person is elevated to love.

Integrity is aligned with honesty and truth, so living your life in integrity will strengthen your throat chakra. This means living your life honestly, within a certain structure that supports your divine self. Be open and honest in relationships, both personal and professional. Do to others what you would like them to do to you.

Also, it is very important to live within your means, being honest about what you can and cannot afford. Living outside of financial integrity indicates a need for healing, which in most cases will lead you back to your inner child in the sacral chakra. Gambling addictions and credit card debt need to be looked at with an open and honest appraisal of your lifestyle.

Harness your will power to make your life the best that it can be. Back yourself, and believe in yourself—you are capable of creating a most magnificent life. Begin today!

Here are some positive affirmations for the throat chakra:

I choose to live my life openly and honestly, in integrity.
Truth is my friend; it frees my soul.
I speak my truth, and the divine creator listens.
I trust in myself; my truth is aligned with my soul.
My communication is honest; people hear my truth.

The third eye chakra is the control centre and our seat of wisdom. Ideas and inspiration are distilled in this energy centre. Thoughts are processed and dreams created. In its strongest state, it stimulates both hemispheres of the brain, creating a psychologically mature, ethical, and philosophical mindset.

It is here in the third eye chakra that strong positive beliefs about ourselves make us resilient to the disruptions of the world around us. It has been said that the power of the mind creates our reality. In the realm of the mind, we dream and harness our internal guidance system. The power and practice of positive thinking can create the world we want to live in. So if we focus our intellect on what is good for us, we make positive choices to enhance this.

The imagination is a powerful tool that is harnessed in the third eye. Using your "mind's eye" to daydream and plan your future makes the reality of a wonderful future more possible. You can use the power of your mind to heal yourself, to get that job—to take charge of your well-being. The practice of creative visualisation will strengthen your meditations and your connection to your spirit guide. All of this activity sits in the third eye.

Reading inspirational books and educating yourself helps you decide on life choices that feel right. You must cultivate an interest in expanding your mind, and be an independent thinker. Sharing quality time with like-minded and inspiring people will also help.

Your spirit guide can show you things through your third eye. As this chakra is connected to the auditory system, you may become able to hear the divine words that your spirit guide speaks to you.

Here are some positive affirmations to support the third eye chakra:

I am open and receptive to divine inspiration.
I am the master of my thoughts.
I choose to see the world through the power of light.
What I think, I become; my life is in my hands.
I welcome guidance and support from my divine intelligence.

The crown chakra sits just above the physical body and is your spiritual gateway to the Divine Creator. Your spirit guide accesses your energy field at this point and filters your higher-self energy through your crown into your physical dimension. The divine energy in the crown chakra is aligned with feelings of peace, harmony, bliss, and balance.

The goal is always to see the light in yourself as well as others; this is made possible by opening the crown to unconditional love. The crown chakra is supported by meditation, prayers, reflection, and silence. When the chakra system is in balance, the crown chakra is fully aligned with divine light and love.

During meditation the crown opens up, and the spiritual body moves into a higher dimension and connects to spiritual guidance. During this process the physical body relaxes and rests. At the close of meditation, it is important to become fully aware in the physical, ensuring your spiritual body is aligned with your physical body and you feel "grounded."

To support the full development of the crown chakra, it is recommended that you listen to beautiful music and read enlightening books and literature. Again, it is good to spend time with people who affirm your divinity and respect you on all levels.

Here are some positive affirmations to support the crown chakra:

I lovingly accept and honour myself on all levels of my existence.
I welcome divine guidance and inspiration.
My life is a representation of divine will,
allowing my inherent gifts to flow.
I choose to bring goodness into my life and into the lives of others.
I am guided to the best outcomes always, for my highest good.

As you continue to take time for self-refection and meditation, you will ensure a balance in life that supports your personal and spiritual journey. When all energy centres are balanced and in harmony with each other, then it is possible to manifest personal goals, as well as true joy, abundant flow, purpose, and personal satisfaction.

Your life goals need to be aligned with your personal truth before you will manifest these goals in your reality. In turn, your personal truth must be aligned with energy of the Creator and your authentic self for the outcome to be for your highest good.

What you truly believe and know about yourself will be paramount in the unfolding of your life.

19

Find a place inside where there is joy and the joy will burn out the pain.

JOSEPH CAMPBELL
(1904–1987, AMERICAN PROFESSOR OF LITERATURE)

Joy and Happiness

As souls, we live our lives according to what we know and what we feel. I truly believe that in any given moment we will choose what is for our highest good. It makes sense. Why would we choose otherwise? However, we respond to our circumstances in every moment through our chakra systems, our memory stores, and our emotional states. We choose our directions and our actions based on what we think is right and good. But what if our judgement is clouded and confused? What if, when we are making a decision, the emotion of what we are feeling is based on traumatic experience, personal pain, or even fear?

The most impacting energy from which we function daily comes through the emotional body. Emotions will usually override the rational mind, especially if these emotions are fear-based. Planet

Earth is an emotional planet, and it is through the healing of our emotions and feelings that we can transcend to higher realms of existence.

Negative traits in people weigh more heavily than positive ones. They keep us feeling low, disempowered, and stuck. The problem is that negative emotions—such as sadness, despair, fear, frustration, jealousy, anxiety, sorrow, and greed—keep us on a treadmill going around and around and getting nowhere fast.

Positive traits—such as kindness, generosity, courage, humility, excitement, abundance, and compassion—allow our energetic vibration to soar. They bring us up and allow us to have fun and enjoy our days. The difficulty comes in the fact that our world is so full of negativity that it is too easy to be pulled back into the quagmire of emotional pain and hopelessness.

In the words of Napoleon Hill, "If you cannot do great things, do small things well."

We must all start somewhere.

In our world, we follow the pursuit of happiness. From my observations, happiness can be a nice meal, new shoes, a funny movie, or a satisfying day at work. Happiness comes to us in many ways. What makes you happy?

I think that when answering this question, many people will talk about things they love to do, buy, or eat. These things are often superficial, and they feed an aspect of our emotional bodies that resonates at "happy." I believe happiness has lost it meaning over time, because we have been told by marketing agencies, social media, and other forms of media what it is that we need in order to feel happy. If we do not have what it is we are told we need, we feel disappointment, frustration, self-pity, unhappiness—and the negative emotional list goes on.

I said in an earlier chapter that it doesn't matter how much you own or have in the material world if you are not happy on the inside. On my personal journey as a spiritual healer, I have met many unhappy people who have money, prestige, social position, and wealth. We need to shift the paradigm and make happiness available to everyone.

Anne Frank said, "Whoever is happy will make others happy too." Happiness is a beautiful energy that can be shared. If only it could be harnessed for all!

Meditation and time spent in the loving energy of your spirit guide will make you happy. In fact, you will experience the higher vibration of happiness which is *joy*.

Joy is a wonderful, fleeting feeling that is difficult to hold onto. It moves from your sacral chakra and flows into your heart, unexpectedly, when everything in your life lines up in positive ways at the same time. It is a moment when everything is perfect and right, and you experience the warmth of this exquisite energy moving through every cell of your body.

Joy is usually unplanned; it just happens! It is in us and can be unleashed in special moments, when if we are still and aware, we will feel it.

I am sure you have all experienced joy at some point in your life. Why don't you take a moment now to reflect on joy and what it means to you? Spend a moment or two remembering that time and feeling the joy.

Children are joyful. They exude this energy with ease. The emotional bodies of children are clearer and more aligned with truth and love. Watching children at play can bring feelings of joy. I have recently spent time with my four-month-old grandson. His smile and laughter are enough to fill my heart with joy.

People can also be joyful by nature. Joy resonates through them and is contagious. It is their way of existence and is not tied in to material wealth or financial abundance. Joyful souls just *are*. They are untroubled and full of life. In my opinion, the Dalai Lama is a human embodiment of joy. It shines through his eyes. His laughter is contagious, and so is his smile!

Happiness is more easily attained. Happiness is aligned with our physical and material world. Happiness sits in the heart chakra. It vibrates at green, the colour of our natural world, our grass, and our trees. It is the Divine Creator's reminder of the love we can exist in on earth.

Joy is a divine energy that comes from within our souls. It's a fleeting memory of pure perfection and unconditional love. It takes us, in a moment, back to our origins, to the origins of our souls. As we open our hearts to our spirit guides, we will open to the true potential of our souls. Joy and happiness are inherent in the energy of the Divine, and we are entitled to all that is on offer to us!

Happiness is not a goal ... it's a by-product of a life well lived.

ELEANOR ROOSEVELT
(1884–1962, FORMER FIRST LADY OF THE UNITED STATES.)

Allow yourself to be joyful; allow yourself to be happy.

20

Personal transformation can and does have a global effect.
As we go, so goes the world; the world is us. The revolution
that will save the world is ultimately a personal one.

MARIANNE WILLIAMSON

Living Inspirit

Earth is our home for now. It is where we were born and where we will die. Our legacy can be one of light and love, if we choose it. It is never too late to embrace love, kindness, and hope. With healing we can forgive ourselves and others. With healing we can transmute negative energy and have it converted to positive energy for Mother Earth. We do this with the help of our spirit guides and the angelic presence that is aligned with us to assist.

Being a light worker is not difficult. It is simply someone who works with light! As you clear the deep, dark aspects of your emotional body, light will enter. Your spirit guide will ensure this is so. Your physical body will fill with light; every cell of your body can shift to a higher vibration. Once the negativity is released, light will improve your physical, emotional, mental, and etheric bodies.

As you manage your thoughts and internal dialogue, you will make more positive choices each day. As you surround yourself with like-minded and loving, trustworthy people, your heart will grow in love and your physical vitality will soar. Simply by choosing a better way to live your life, in alignment with your spiritual self, you will move mountains. Miracles can happen—anything and everything *good* is possible.

I began my journey of introspection and spiritual growth many years ago. It was a solitary journey for a very long time. It is sometimes hard to find like-minded souls who "get" you. This didn't bother me at all. In fact, I believe your spirituality is a very personal thing. Your connection to the creator of your soul is supremely personal. I identified aspects of myself that I didn't like. Learning to love these parts of me was difficult and not something I wanted to share. We are entitled to a private and sacred world. Only when we feel we are in the right company, do we truly feel safe in opening up our personal thoughts and feelings.

I believe that the communication with our spirit guides is the ultimate gift on this journey and with this gift, comes the opportunity to grow spiritually and heal ourselves.

Underlying every disease is an emotional, negative vibration that, if left unaddressed, will fester into chronic pain or illness. We can all become healthier and whole, simply by acknowledging the power of love and light. This energy diminishes sadness, ill health, grief, anger, hopelessness, and despair.

Why would anyone turn his back on an opportunity to live a better life—especially when the path is simple and easily accessed?

A path of healing, energy, and light is available to all. It is through this pathway that we can find happiness and sustenance for our souls. Our souls need to grow; that is why we are here on earth. As our souls grow in light and love, we assist in raising the vibration of our earthly home. The acorn grows into the magnificent tree of life, and the Garden of Eden flourishes yet again.

No one lights a lamp in order to hide it behind a door: the purpose of light is to create more light, to open people's eyes to reveal the marvels around.

———

PAUL COELHO
(1947–PRESENT, BRAZILIAN NOVELIST)

Our world is moving towards a place of new endeavour, a place of hard work but also progress and sustainability. As light workers, we share our environment with other soul energies that coexist in harmony, under the common goal of brotherhood, sisterhood, and good living. Our light community can strive forward to be the best that we can be, supporting and sharing love for each other.

The Quiet Light Revolution is happening all around us. Light is an energy, and through the connection to your spirit guide, you can access this energy every day for the rest of your life. The choice is yours, and if you choose, you will make a difference. The difference you make will be positive and good. With light, you can align with universal love. Love and light go hand in hand.

Love opens the door for the light to shine through.

The higher self of each soul is the closest aspect to unconditional love, and the Creator, that we can physically experience here on earth. The higher self takes us back to the source of all that is. This flowing down of love and light nurtures our souls, but more than that, it fills us with the wisdom of the Creator. Within this energy of love, light, and eternal wisdom, anything is possible. This is where miracles can happen.

Through a dedicated practice of meditation and commitment to bringing light into your world, *you* can bring about change. All it takes is a comfortable chair, a journal, and a pen. Imagine being able to change the world from the comfort of your own home! This is truly possible. There is no need to join a large group meditation, or a sacred circle, or climb a mountain to Tibet. There is, in fact, no need to join a group consciousness at all. You definitely do not need a Guru. By aligning in the light through your spirit guide and higher self, you will access an extremely high vibration of pure love and light energy, without the contamination and the dense energy of earth's New Age castoffs.

Humanity has traditionally found spirituality through organised religion. By *Living Inspirit* we are changing this mindset completely. You can be a spiritual person, living in the light, and no one even has to know. Not that we have anything to hide. On the contrary, we shine light everywhere we go! It is just that spirituality is personal, sacred, and profound. Understanding your connection to the Divine Creator is overwhelmingly special and truly all that you need.

Many people find comfort and companionship within organised religion and spiritual group practice. These people enjoy the proximity to their soulmates and friends. However, true spirituality is your unique and individual alignment with the God force within your heart. If you can find this within yourself, you will want for nothing.

Group gatherings merge energy fields, so the larger the group the more lost your energy becomes. When you leave such a gathering, your chakra system will be accessed by cords and people that you will need to clear. The energy of the light worker can be easily drained in these circumstances.

The entire premise of this book is to help you build and protect your energy so that your vibration increases and you become more and more aligned with the Divine Creator within.

The traditional spiritual teachers of the past, and many of the present, carry a similar message. God is separate from us. God is masculine. God must forgive us before we are embraced by his love. So, let us in the simplest of ways, change this around. Let us bring forth the Divine Creator energy, which is both male and female in origin, from within our soul selves and our hearts.

Consider these daily affirmations:

**The divine creator of all that is exists
within every cell of my body.
I love myself unconditionally, and I choose to be a vessel of light.
I forgive myself on all levels of my existence, now and forever.**

The journey into the light is a process of becoming self-aware; it is a journey of self-knowledge and a journey of introspection. All it requires is a commitment and a willingness to change for the better. When you choose light, you choose love. And with this love and light, the dark pockets of life's difficult struggles will disappear. You will gain strength in your emotional body and be able to take life head-on, with a positive *can-do* attitude and faith in yourself.

The light you build will have a positive impact on you and on your closest family and friends. The impact is like the pebble in the stream, as the waves of love and hope move through the hearts of those you love.

This is how we, as a connected group of like-minded souls, will make a difference. This is how we will replant the Garden of Eden with new life, new positive energy, and light. We will initiate new hope for our earthly home, shining the light to all who seek a better life. In this energy the innate goodness of our world will prevail, and it will be a home to loving beings in the generations to come.

This is our truth.

This is the Quiet Light Revolution!

Printed in the United States
By Bookmasters